ON THESE I STAND

On These I Stand

An Anthology of the Best Poems

of

COUNTEE CULLEN

———

Selected by Himself and Including Six
New Poems Never Before Published

———

HARPER & BROTHERS PUBLISHERS

New York and London

This book is for my wife

Ida M. Cullen

Contents

[vii]

From COPPER SUN

From THE BLACK CHRIST

[x]

FROM

COLOR

━━

Yet Do I Marvel

I DOUBT not God is good, well-meaning, kind,
And did He stoop to quibble could tell why
The little buried mole continues blind,
Why flesh that mirrors Him must some day die,
Make plain the reason tortured Tantalus
Is baited by the fickle fruit, declare
If merely brute caprice dooms Sisyphus
To struggle up a never-ending stair.
Inscrutable His ways are, and immune
To catechism by a mind too strewn
With petty cares to slightly understand
What awful brain compels His awful hand.
Yet do I marvel at this curious thing:
To make a poet black, and bid him sing!

A Song of Praise

(For one who praised his lady's being fair.)

You have not heard my love's dark throat,
    Slow-fluting like a reed,
Release the perfect golden note
    She caged there for my need.

Her walk is like the replica
    Of some barbaric dance
Wherein the soul of Africa
    Is winged with arrogance.

And yet so light she steps across
    The ways her sure feet pass,
She does not dent the smoothest moss
    Or bend the thinnest grass.

My love is dark as yours is fair,
    Yet lovelier I hold her
Than listless maids with pallid hair,
    And blood that's thin and colder.

You-proud-and-to-be-pitied one,
    Gaze on her and despair;
Then seal your lips until the sun
    Discovers one as fair.

A Brown Girl Dead

WITH two white roses on her breasts,
   White candles at head and feet,
Dark Madonna of the grave she rests;
   Lord Death has found her sweet.

Her mother pawned her wedding ring
   To lay her out in white;
She'd be so proud she'd dance and sing
   To see herself tonight.

Black Magdalens

THESE have no Christ to spit and stoop
   To write upon the sand,
Inviting him that has not sinned
   To raise the first rude hand.

And if he came they could not buy
   Rich ointment for his feet,
The body's sale scarce yields enough
   To let the body eat.

The chaste clean ladies pass them by
   And draw their skirts aside,
But Magdalens have a ready laugh;
   They wrap their wounds in pride.

They fare full ill since Christ forsook
   The cross to mount a throne,
And Virtue still is stooping down
   To cast the first hard stone.

Tableau

(For Donald Duff)

LOCKED arm in arm they cross the way,
  The black boy and the white,
The golden splendor of the day,
  The sable pride of night.

From lowered blinds the dark folk stare,
  And here the fair folk talk,
Indignant that these two should dare
  In unison to walk.

Oblivious to look and word
  They pass, and see no wonder
That lightning brilliant as a sword
  Should blaze the path of thunder.

Simon the Cyrenian Speaks

HE never spoke a word to me,
  And yet He called my name;
He never gave a sign to me,
  And yet I knew and came.

At first I said, "I will not bear
  His cross upon my back;
He only seeks to place it there
  Because my skin is black."

But He was dying for a dream,
  And He was very meek,
And in His eyes there shone a gleam
  Men journey far to seek.

It was Himself my pity bought;
  I did for Christ alone
What all of Rome could not have wrought
  With bruise of lash or stone.

Incident

(*For Eric Walrond*)

ONCE riding in old Baltimore,
    Heart-filled, head-filled with glee,
I saw a Baltimorean
    Keep looking straight at me.

Now I was eight and very small,
    And he was no whit bigger,
And so I smiled, but he poked out
    His tongue, and called me, "Nigger."

I saw the whole of Baltimore
    From May until December;
Of all the things that happened there
    That's all that I remember.

Saturday's Child

SOME are teethed on a silver spoon,
  With the stars strung for a rattle;
I cut my teeth as the black raccoon—
  For implements of battle.

Some are swaddled in silk and down,
  And heralded by a star;
They swathed my limbs in a sackcloth gown
  On a night that was black as tar.

For some, godfather and goddame
  The opulent fairies be;
Dame Poverty gave me my name,
  And Pain godfathered me.

For I was born on Saturday—
  "Bad time for planting a seed,"
Was all my father had to say,
  And, "One mouth more to feed."

Death cut the strings that gave me life,
  And handed me to Sorrow,
The only kind of middle wife
  My folks could beg or borrow.

Pagan Prayer

Not for myself I make this prayer,
    But for this race of mine
That stretches forth from shadowed places
    Dark hands for bread and wine.

For me, my heart is pagan mad,
    My feet are never still,
But give them hearths to keep them warm
    In homes high on a hill.

For me, my faith lies fallowing,
    I bow not till I see,
But these are humble and believe;
    Bless their credulity.

For me, I pay my debts in kind,
    And see no better way,
Bless these who turn the other cheek
    For love of you, and pray.

Our Father, God, our Brother, Christ—
    So are we taught to pray;
Their kinship seems a little thing
    Who sorrow all the day.

Our Father, God; our Brother, Christ,
    Or are we bastard kin,
That to our plaints your ears are closed,
    Your doors barred from within?

Our Father, God; our Brother, Christ,
Retrieve my race again;
So shall you compass this black sheep,
This pagan heart. Amen.

Wisdom Cometh With the Years

Now I am young and credulous,
  My heart is quick to bleed
At courage in the tremulous
  Slow sprouting of a seed.

Now I am young and sensitive,
  Man's lack can stab me through;
I own no stitch I would not give
  To him that asked me to.

Now I am young and a fool for love,
  My blood goes mad to see
A brown girl pass me like a dove
  That flies melodiously.

Let me be lavish of my tears,
  And dream that false is true;
Though wisdom cometh with the years,
  The barren days come, too.

Fruit of the Flower

MY father is a quiet man
    With sober, steady ways;
For simile, a folded fan;
    His nights are like his days.

My mother's life is puritan,
    No hint of cavalier,
A pool so calm you're sure it can
    Have little depth to fear.

And yet my father's eyes can boast
    How full his life has been;
There haunts them yet the languid ghost
    Of some still sacred sin.

And though my mother chants of God,
    And of the mystic river,
I've seen a bit of checkered sod
    Set all her flesh aquiver.

Why should he deem it pure mischance
    A son of his is fain
To do a naked tribal dance
    Each time he hears the rain?

Why should she think it devil's art
    That all my songs should be
Of love and lovers, broken heart,
    And wild sweet agony?

[14]

Who plants a seed begets a bud,
Extract of that same root;
Why marvel at the hectic blood
That flushes this wild fruit?

The Shroud of Color

(For Llewellyn Ransom)

LORD, being dark," I said, "I cannot bear
The further touch of earth, the scented air;
Lord, being dark, forewilled to that despair
My color shrouds me in, I am as dirt
Beneath my brother's heel; there is a hurt
In all the simple joys which to a child
Are sweet; they are contaminate, defiled
By truths of wrongs the childish vision fails
To see; too great a cost this birth entails.
I strangle in this yoke drawn tighter than
The worth of bearing it, just to be man.
I am not brave enough to pay the price
In full; I lack the strength to sacrifice.
I who have burned my hands upon a star,
And climbed high hills at dawn to view the far
Illimitable wonderments of earth,
For whom all cups have dripped the wine of mirth,
For whom the sea has strained her honeyed throat
Till all the world was sea, and I a boat
Unmoored, on what strange quest I willed to float;
Who wore a many-colored coat of dreams,
Thy gift, O Lord—I whom sun-dabbled streams
Have washed, whose bare brown thighs have held the sun
Incarcerate until his course was run,
I who considered man a high-perfected
Glass where loveliness could lie reflected,

Now that I sway athwart Truth's deep abyss,
Denuding man for what he was and is,
Shall breath and being so inveigle me
That I can damn my dreams to hell, and be
Content, each new-born day, anew to see
The steaming crimson vintage of my youth
Incarnadine the altar-slab of Truth?

Or hast Thou, Lord, somewhere I cannot see,
A lamb imprisoned in a bush for me?

Not so? Then let me render one by one
Thy gifts, while still they shine; some little sun
Yet gilds these thighs; my coat, albeit worn,
Still hold its colors fast; albeit torn,
My heart will laugh a little yet, if I
May win of Thee this grace, Lord: on this high
And sacrificial hill 'twixt earth and sky,
To dream still pure all that I loved, and die.
There is no other way to keep secure
My wild chimeras; grave-locked against the lure
Of Truth, the small hard teeth of worms, yet less
Envenomed than the mouth of Truth, will bless
Them into dust and happy nothingness.
Lord, Thou art God; and I, Lord, what am I
But dust? With dust my place. Lord, let me die."

Across the earth's warm, palpitating crust
I flung my body in embrace; I thrust
My mouth into the grass and sucked the dew,
Then gave it back in tears my anguish drew;

[17]

So hard I pressed against the ground, I felt
The smallest sandgrain like a knife, and smelt
The next year's flowering; all this to speed
My body's dissolution, fain to feed
The worms. And so I groaned, and spent my strength
Until, all passion spent, I lay full length
And quivered like a flayed and bleeding thing.

So lay till lifted on a great black wing
That had no mate nor flesh-apparent trunk
To hamper it; with me all time had sunk
Into oblivion; when I awoke
The wing hung poised above two cliffs that broke
The bowels of the earth in twain, and cleft
The seas apart. Below, above, to left,
To right, I saw what no man saw before:
Earth, hell, and heaven; sinew, vein, and core.
All things that swim or walk or creep or fly,
All things that live and hunger, faint and die,
Were made majestic then and magnified
By sight so clearly purged and deified.
The smallest bug that crawls was taller than
A tree, the mustard seed loomed like a man.
The earth that writhes eternally with pain
Of birth, and woe of taking back her slain,
Laid bare her teeming bosom to my sight,
And all was struggle, gasping breath, and fight.
A blind worm here dug tunnels to the light,
And there a seed, racked with heroic pain,
Thrust eager tentacles to sun and rain;

It climbed; it died; the old love conquered me
To weep the blossom it would never be.
But here a bud won light; it burst and flowered
Into a rose whose beauty challenged, "Coward!"
There was no thing alive save only I
That held life in contempt and longed to die.
And still I writhed and moaned, "The curse, the curse,
Than animated death, can death be worse?"

*"Dark child of sorrow, mine no less, what art
Of mine can make thee see and play thy part?
The key to all strange things is in thy heart."*

What voice was this that coursed like liquid fire
Along my flesh, and turned my hair to wire?

I raised my burning eyes, beheld a field
All multitudinous with carnal yield,
A grim ensanguined mead whereon I saw
Evolve the ancient fundamental law
Of tooth and talon, fist and nail and claw.
There with the force of living, hostile hills
Whose clash the hemmed-in vale with clamor fills,
With greater din contended fierce majestic wills
Of beast with beast, of man with man, in strife
For love of what my heart despised, for life
That unto me at dawn was now a prayer
For night, at night a bloody heart-wrung tear
For day again; for *this*, these groans
From tangled flesh and interlockèd bones.

And no thing died that did not give
A testimony that it longed to live.
Man, strange composite blend of brute and god,
Pushed on, nor backward glanced where last he trod.
He seemed to mount a misty ladder flung
Pendant from a cloud, yet never gained a rung
But at his feet another tugged and clung.
My heart was still a pool of bitterness,
Would yield nought else, nought else confess.
I spoke (although no form was there
To see, I knew an ear was there to hear),
"Well, let them fight; they *can* whose flesh is fair."

Crisp lightning flashed; a wave of thunder shook
My wing; a pause, and then a speaking, "Look."

I scarce dared trust my ears or eyes for awe
Of what they heard, and dread of what they saw;
For, privileged beyond degree, this flesh
Beheld God and His heaven in the mesh
Of Lucifer's revolt, saw Lucifer
Glow like the sun, and like a dulcimer
I heard his sin-sweet voice break on the yell
Of God's great warriors: Gabriel,
Saint Clair and Michael, Israfel and Raphael.
And strange it was to see God with His back
Against a wall, to see Christ hew and hack
Till Lucifer, pressed by the mighty pair,
And losing inch by inch, clawed at the air
With fevered wings; then, lost beyond repair,
He tricked a mass of stars into his hair;

He filled his hands with stars, crying as he fell,
"A star's a star although it burns in hell."
So God was left to His divinity,
Omnipotent at that most costly fee.

There was a lesson here, but still the clod
In me was sycophant unto the rod,
And cried, "Why mock me thus? Am I a god?"

*"One trial more: this failing, then I give
You leave to die; no further need to live."*

Now suddenly a strange wild music smote
A chord long impotent in me; a note
Of jungles, primitive and subtle, throbbed
Against my echoing breast, and tom-toms sobbed
In every pulse-beat of my frame. The din
A hollow log bound with a python's skin
Can make wrought every nerve to ecstasy,
And I was wind and sky again, and sea,
And all sweet things that flourish, being free.

Till all at once the music changed its key.

And now it was of bitterness and death,
The cry the lash extorts, the broken breath
Of liberty enchained; and yet there ran
Through all a harmony of faith in man,
A knowledge all would end as it began.
All sights and sounds and aspects of my race
Accompanied this melody, kept pace

With it; with music all their hopes and hates
Were charged, not to be downed by all the fates.
And somehow it was borne upon my brain
How being dark, and living through the pain
Of it, is courage more than angels have. I knew
What storms and tumults lashed the tree that grew
This body that I was, this cringing I
That feared to contemplate a changing sky,
This that I grovelled, whining, "Let me die,"
While others struggled in Life's abattoir.
The cries of all dark people near or far
Were billowed over me, a mighty surge
Of suffering in which my puny grief must merge
And lose itself; I had no further claim to urge
For death; in shame I raised my dust-grimed head,
And though my lips moved not, God knew I said,
"Lord, not for what I saw in flesh or bone
Of fairer men; not raised on faith alone;
Lord, I will live persuaded by mine own.
I cannot play the recreant to these;
My spirit has come home, that sailed the doubtful seas."
With the whiz of a sword that severs space,
The wing dropped down at a dizzy pace,
And flung me on my hill flat on my face;
Flat on my face I lay defying pain,
Glad of the blood in my smallest vein,
And in my hands I clutched a loyal dream,
Still spitting fire, bright twist and coil and gleam,
And chiselled like a hound's white tooth.
"Oh, I will match you yet," I cried, "to truth."

Right glad I was to stoop to what I once had spurned,
Glad even unto tears; I laughed aloud; I turned
Upon my back, and though the tears for joy would run,
My sight was clear; I looked and saw the rising sun.

Heritage

(*For Harold Jackman*)

WHAT is Africa to me:
Copper sun or scarlet sea,
Jungle star or jungle track,
Strong bronzed men, or regal black
Women from whose loins I sprang
When the birds of Eden sang?
One three centuries removed
From the scenes his fathers loved,
Spicy grove, cinnamon tree,
What is Africa to me?

So I lie, who all day long
Want no sound except the song
Sung by wild barbaric birds
Goading massive jungle herds,
Juggernauts of flesh that pass
Trampling tall defiant grass
Where young forest lovers lie,
Plighting troth beneath the sky.
So I lie, who always hear,
Though I cram against my ear
Both my thumbs, and keep them there,
Great drums throbbing through the air.
So I lie, whose fount of pride,
Dear distress, and joy allied,

Is my somber flesh and skin,
With the dark blood dammed within
Like great pulsing tides of wine
That, I fear, must burst the fine
Channels of the chafing net
Where they surge and foam and fret.

Africa? A book one thumbs
Listlessly, till slumber comes.
Unremembered are her bats
Circling through the night, her cats
Crouching in the river reeds,
Stalking gentle flesh that feeds
By the river brink; no more
Does the bugle-throated roar
Cry that monarch claws have leapt
From the scabbards where they slept.
Silver snakes that once a year
Doff the lovely coats you wear,
Seek no covert in your fear
Lest a mortal eye should see;
What's your nakedness to me?
Here no leprous flowers rear
Fierce corollas in the air;
Here no bodies sleek and wet,
Dripping mingled rain and sweat,
Tread the savage measures of
Jungle boys and girls in love.
What is last year's snow to me,
Last year's anything? The tree

Budding yearly must forget
How its past arose or set—
Bough and blossom, flower, fruit,
Even what shy bird with mute
Wonder at her travail there,
Meekly labored in its hair.
One three centuries removed
From the scenes his fathers loved,
Spicy grove, cinnamon tree,
What is Africa to me?

So I lie, who find no peace
Night or day, no slight release
From the unremittant beat
Made by cruel padded feet
Walking through my body's street.
Up and down they go, and back,
Treading out a jungle track.
So I lie, who never quite
Safely sleep from rain at night—
I can never rest at all
When the rain begins to fall;
Like a soul gone mad with pain
I must match its weird refrain;
Ever must I twist and squirm,
Writhing like a baited worm,
While its primal measures drip
Through my body, crying, "Strip!
Doff this new exuberance.
Come and dance the Lover's Dance!"

In an old remembered way
Rain works on me night and day.

Quaint, outlandish heathen gods
Black men fashion out of rods,
Clay, and brittle bits of stone,
In a likeness like their own,
My conversion came high-priced;
I belong to Jesus Christ,
Preacher of humility;
Heathen gods are naught to me.

Father, Son, and Holy Ghost,
So I make an idle boast;
Jesus of the twice-turned cheek,
Lamb of God, although I speak
With my mouth thus, in my heart
Do I play a double part.
Ever at Thy glowing altar
Must my heart grow sick and falter,
Wishing He I served were black,
Thinking then it would not lack
Precedent of pain to guide it,
Let who would or might deride it;
Surely then this flesh would know
Yours had borne a kindred woe.
Lord, I fashion dark gods, too,
Daring even to give You
Dark despairing features where,
Crowned with dark rebellious hair,

Patience wavers just so much as
Mortal grief compels, while touches
Quick and hot, of anger, rise
To smitten cheek and weary eyes.
Lord, forgive me if my need
Sometimes shapes a human creed.
All day long and all night through,
One thing only must I do:
Quench my pride and cool my blood,
Lest I perish in the flood.
Lest a hidden ember set
Timber that I thought was wet
Burning like the dryest flax,
Melting like the merest wax,
Lest the grave restore its dead.
Not yet has my heart or head
In the least way realized
They and I are civilized.

EPITAPHS

For a Poet

I HAVE wrapped my dreams in a silken cloth,
And laid them away in a box of gold;
Where long will cling the lips of the moth,
I have wrapped my dreams in a silken cloth;
I hide no hate; I am not even wroth
Who found earth's breath so keen and cold;
I have wrapped my dreams in a silken cloth,
And laid them away in a box of gold.

For My Grandmother

THIS lovely flower fell to seed;
  Work gently, sun and rain;
She held it as her dying creed
  That she would grow again.

For a Lady I Know

SHE even thinks that up in heaven
    Her class lies late and snores,
While poor black cherubs rise at seven
    To do celestial chores.

For a Pessimist

HE wore his coffin for a hat,
　　Calamity his cape,
While on his face a death's-head sat
　　And waved a bit of crape.

For a Mouthy Woman

GOD and the devil still are wrangling
  Which should have her, which repel;
God wants no discord in his heaven;
  Satan has enough in hell.

For John Keats,
Apostle of Beauty

NOT writ in water, nor in mist,
Sweet lyric throat, thy name;
Thy singing lips that cold death kissed
Have seared his own with flame.

For Paul Laurence Dunbar

BORN of the sorrowful of heart,
　Mirth was a crown upon his head;
Pride kept his twisted lips apart
　In jest, to hide a heart that bled.

If You Should Go

LOVE, leave me like the light,
The gently passing day;
We would not know, but for the night,
When it has slipped away.

Go quietly; a dream,
When done, should leave no trace
That it has lived, except a gleam
Across the dreamer's face.

She of the Dancing Feet Sings
(*To Ottie Graham*)

AND what would I do in heaven, pray,
   Me with my dancing feet,
And limbs like apple boughs that sway
   When the gusty rain winds beat?

And how would I thrive in a perfect place
   Where dancing would be sin,
With not a man to love my face,
   Nor an arm to hold me in?

The seraphs and the cherubim
   Would be too proud to bend
To sing the faery tunes that brim
   My heart from end to end.

The wistful angels down in hell
   Will smile to see my face,
And understand, because they fell
   From that all-perfect place.

The Wise

(For *Alain Locke*)

DEAD men are wisest, for they know
How far the roots of flowers go,
How long a seed must rot to grow.

Dead men alone bear frost and rain
On throbless heart and heatless brain,
And feel no stir of joy or pain.

Dead men alone are satiate;
They sleep and dream and have no weight,
To curb their rest, of love or hate.

Strange, men should flee their company,
Or think me strange who long to be
Wrapped in their cool immunity.

To John Keats, Poet
At Spring Time*
(For Carl Van Vechten)

I CANNOT hold my peace, John Keats;
There never was a spring like this;
It is an echo, that repeats
My last year's song and next year's bliss.
I know, in spite of all men say
Of Beauty, you have felt her most.
Yea, even in your grave her way
Is laid. Poor, troubled, lyric ghost,
Spring never was so fair and dear
As Beauty makes her seem this year.

I cannot hold my peace, John Keats,
I am as helpless in the toil
Of Spring as any lamb that bleats
To feel the solid earth recoil
Beneath his puny legs. Spring beats
Her tocsin call to those who love her,
And lo! the dogwood petals cover
Her breast with drifts of snow, and sleek
White gulls fly screaming to her, and hover
About her shoulders, and kiss her cheek,
While white and purple lilacs muster
A strength that bears them to a cluster

* Spring, 1924.

Of color and odor; for her sake
All things that slept are now awake.

And you and I, shall we lie still,
John Keats, while Beauty summons us?
Somehow I feel your sensitive will
Is pulsing up some tremulous
Sap road of a maple tree, whose leaves
Grow music as they grow, since your
Wild voice is in them, a harp that grieves
For life that opens death's dark door.
Though dust, your fingers still can push
The Vision Splendid to a birth,
Though now they work as grass in the hush
Of the night on the broad sweet page of the earth.

"John Keats is dead," they say, but I
Who hear your full insistent cry
In bud and blossom, leaf and tree,
Know John Keats still writes poetry.
And while my head is earthward bowed
To read new life sprung from your shroud,
Folks seeing me must think it strange
That merely spring should so derange
My mind. They do not know that you,
John Keats, keep revel with me, too.

Requiescam

I AM for sleeping and forgetting
All that has gone before;
I am for lying still and letting
Who will beat at my door;
I would my life's cold sun were setting
To rise for me no more.

COPPER SUN

From the Dark Tower

(To Charles S. Johnson)

WE shall not always plant while others reap
The golden increment of bursting fruit,
Not always countenance, abject and mute,
That lesser men should hold their brothers cheap;
Not everlastingly while others sleep
Shall we beguile their limbs with mellow flute,
Not always bend to some more subtle brute;
We were not made eternally to weep.

The night whose sable breast relieves the stark,
White stars is no less lovely being dark,
And there are buds that cannot bloom at all
In light, but crumple, piteous, and fall;
So in the dark we hide the heart that bleeds,
And wait, and tend our agonizing seeds.

Threnody for a Brown Girl

WEEP not, you who love her;
What rebellious flow
Grief undams shall recover
Whom the gods bid go?
Sorrow rising like a wall,
Bitter, blasphemous,
What avails it to recall
Beauty back to us?

Think not this grave shall keep her,
This marriage-bed confine;
Death may dig it deep and deeper;
She shall climb it like a vine.
Body that was quick and sentient,
Dear as thought or speech,
Death could not with one trenchant
Blow snatch out of reach.

She is nearer than the word
Wasted on her now,
Nearer than the swaying bird
On its rhythmic bough.
Only were our faith as much
As a mustard seed,
Aching, hungry hands might touch
Her as they touch a reed.

Life who was not loth to trade her
Unto death, has done
Better than he planned, has made her
Wise as Solomon.
Now she knows the Why and Wherefore,
Troublous Whence and Whither,
Why men strive and sweat, and care for
Bays that droop and wither.

All the stars she knows by name,
End and origin thereof,
Knows if love be kin to shame,
If shame be less than love.
What was crooked now is straight,
What was rough is plain;
Grief and sorrow have no weight
Now to cause her pain.

Plain to her why fevered blisters
Made her dark hands run,
While her favored, fairer sisters
Neither wrought nor spun;
Clear to her the hidden reason
Men daily fret and toil,
Staving death off for a season
Till soil return to soil.

One to her are flame and frost;
Silence is her singing lark;
We alone are children, lost,
Crying in the dark.

Varied feature now, and form,
Change has bred upon her;
Crush no bug nor nauseous worm
Lest you tread upon her.

Pluck no flower lest she scream;
Bruise no slender reed,
Lest it prove more than it seem,
Lest she groan and bleed.
More than ever trust your brother,
Read him golden, pure;
It may be she finds no other
House so safe and sure.

Set no poet carving
Rhymes to make her laugh;
Only live hearts starving
Need an epitaph.
Lay upon her no white stone
From a foreign quarry;
Earth and sky be these alone
Her obituary.

Swift as startled fawn or swallow,
Silence all her sound,
She has fled; we cannot follow
Further than this mound.
We who take the beaten track
Trying to appease
Hearts near breaking with their lack,
We need elegies.

Colors

(*To Leland*)

(Red)

SHE went to buy a brand new hat,
And she was ugly, black, and fat:
"This red becomes you well," they said,
And perched it high upon her head.
And then they laughed behind her back
To see it glow against the black.
She paid for it with regal mien,
And walked out proud as any queen.

(Black)

1

The play is done, the crowds depart; and see
That twisted tortured thing hung from a tree,
Swart victim of a newer Calvary.

2

Yea, he who helped Christ up Golgotha's track,
That Simon who did *not* deny, was black.

(The Unknown Color)

I've often heard my mother say,
When great winds blew across the day,

And, cuddled close and out of sight,
The young pigs squealed with sudden fright
Like something speared or javelined,
"Poor little pigs, they see the wind."

The Litany of the Dark People

prayer

OUR flesh that was a battle-ground
Shows now the morning-break;
The ancient deities are drowned
For Thy eternal sake.
Now that the past is left behind,
Fling wide Thy garment's hem
To keep us one with Thee in mind,
Thou Christ of Bethlehem.

The thorny wreath may ridge our brow,
The spear may mar our side,
And on white wood from a scented bough
We may be crucified;
Yet no assault the old gods make
Upon our agony
Shall swerve our footsteps from the wake
Of Thine toward Calvary.

And if we hunger now and thirst,
Grant our withholders may,
When heaven's constellations burst
Upon Thy crowning day,
Be fed by us, and given to see
Thy mercy in our eyes,
When Bethlehem and Calvary
Are merged in Paradise.

Pity the Deep in Love
(To Fiona)

PITY the deep in love;
They move as men asleep,
Traveling a narrow way
Precipitous and steep.
Tremulous is the lover's breath
With little moans and sighs;
Heavy are the brimming lids
Upon a lover's eyes.

Variations on a Theme
(The Loss of Love)

1

THIS house where Love a little while abode,
Impoverished completely of him now,
Of every vestige bare, drained like a bough
Wherefrom the all-sustaining sap has flowed
Away, yet bears upon its front bestowed
A cabalistic legend telling how
Love for a meagre space deigned to allow
It summer scent before the winter snowed.
Here rots to ruin a splendor proudly calm,
A skeleton whereof the clean bones wear
Their indigence relieved of any qualm
For purple robes that once were folded there.
The mouldy Coliseum draws upon
Our wonder yet . . . no less Love's Parthenon.

2

All through an empty place I go,
And find her not in any room;
The candles and the lamps I light
Go down before a wind of gloom.

Thick-spraddled lies the dust about,
A fit, sad place to write her name
Or draw her face the way she looked
That legendary night she came.

[55]

The old house crumbles bit by bit;
Each day I hear the ominous thud
That says another rent is there
For winds to pierce and storms to flood.

My orchards groan and sag with fruit;
Where, Indian-wise, the bees go round;
I let it rot upon the bough;
I eat what falls upon the ground.

The heavy cows go laboring
In agony with clotted teats;
My hands are slack; my blood is cold;
I marvel that my heart still beats.

I have no will to weep or sing,
No least desire to pray or curse;
The loss of love is a terrible thing;
They lie who say that death is worse.

A Song of Sour Grapes

I WISH your body were in the grave,
Deep down as a grave may be,
Or rotting under the deepest wave
That ever ploughed the sea.

I wish I never had seen your face,
Or the sinuous curve of your mouth,
Dear as a straw to a man who drowns
Or rain to a land in drouth.

I would that your mother had never borne
Your father's seed to fruit,
That meadow rats had gnawed his corn
Before it gathered root.

Lament

Now let all lovely things embark
Upon the sea of mist
With her whose luscious mouth the dark,
Grim troubadour has kissed.

The silver clock that ticked away
Her days, and never knew
Its beats were sword thrusts to the clay
That too much beauty slew.

The pillow favored with her tears
And hallowed by her head;
I shall not even keep my fears,
Now their concern is dead.

But where shall I bury sun and rain,
How mortalise the stars,
How still the half-heard cries of pain
That seared her soul with scars?

In what sea depths shall all the seeds
Of every flower die?
Where shall I scatter the broken reeds,
And how erase the sky?

And where shall I find a hole so deep
No troubled ghost may rise?
There will I put my heart to sleep
Wanting her face and eyes.

[58]

The Love Tree

COME, let us plant our love as farmers plant
A seed, and you shall water it with tears,
And I shall weed it with my hands until
They bleed. Perchance this buried love of ours
Will fall on goodly ground and bear a tree
With fruit and flowers; pale lovers chancing here
May pluck and eat, and through their veins a sweet
And languid ardor play, their pulses beat
An unimagined tune, their shy lips meet
And part, and bliss repeat again. And men
Will pilgrimage from far and wide to see
This tree for which we two were crucified,
And, happy in themselves, will never know
'Twas break of heart that made the Love Tree grow.

Two Thoughts of Death

1

WHEN I am dead, it will not be
Much matter of concern to me
Who folds my hands, or combs my hair,
Or, pitying their sightless stare,
Draws down the blinds across my eyes.
I shall not have the least surmise
Which of the many loves I had
Weeps most the passing of her lad.
Not what these give, nor what they keep,
Shall gladden or disturb my sleep,
If only one who never guessed
How every tremor in her breast
Reverberated in my own.
In that last hour come and bend down
To kiss my long-expectant mouth
Still curved, in death, to meet her mouth.

2

I am content to play the martyr,
To wear the dunce cap here at school;
For every tear I shed I'll barter
To Death; I'll be no more a fool
When that pale rider reaches down
His hand to me. He'll beat a crown
From all the aches my shoulders bore,
And I shall lord one regal hour

Illumined in all things before
His sickle spears another flower.
While still his shears snarl through my thread,
Dismembering it strand by strand,
While I hang poised between the dead
And quick, into omniscience fanned,
My mind shall glow with one rich spark
Before it ends in endless dark.
These straining eyes, clairvoyant then,
Shall probe beneath the calloused husk
That hides the better selves of men.
And as my day throbs into dusk,
This heart the world has made to bleed,
While all its red stream deathward flows,
Shall comprehend just why the seed
Must agonize to be the rose.

Love's Way

LOVE is not love demanding all, itself
Withholding aught; love's is the nobler way
Of courtesy, that will not feast aware
That the beloved hungers, nor drink unless
The cup be shared down to the last sweet dregs.
Renunciatory never was the thorn
To crown love with, but *prodigal* and *proud*!
Too proud to rest the debtor of the one
Dear passion most it dotes upon, always
Love rehabilitates unto the end.
So let it be with us; the perfect faith
We each to other swear this moment leaves
Our scales harmonious, neither wanting found
Though weighed in such strict balances. So let
It be with us always. I am too proud
To owe you one caress; you must not drop
Beholden to my favor for one least
Endearing term. Should you reveal some stretch
Of sky to me, let me revive some note
Of music lost to you. This is love's way,
That where a heart is asked gives back a heart.

Cor Cordium*

COR *cordium* is written there,
But the heart of hearts is away;
They could not fashion any bier
To hold that burning clay.

Imprisoned in the flesh, he wrought
Till Death as Prospero,
Pitied the spark that life had caught,
Loosed him, and let him go.

Look, a light like a sun-girt flask;
Listen, and hear it sing.
Light and song are what, you ask?
Ariel off on the wing!

* Written at the Shelly Memorial in Rome, August 1926.

Protest

(To John Trounstine)

I LONG not now, a little while at least,
For that serene interminable hour
When I shall leave this Barmecidal feast
With poppy for my everlasting flower;
I long not now for that dim cubicle
Of earth to which my lease will not expire,
Where he who comes a tenant there may dwell
Without a thought of famine, flood, or fire.

Surely that house has quiet to bestow—
Still tongue, spent pulse, heart pumped of its last throb,
The fingers tense and tranquil in a row,
The throat unwelled with any sigh or sob—
But time to live, to love, bear pain and smile,
Oh, we are given such a little while!

Youth Sings a Song of Rosebuds

(*To Roberta*)

SINCE men grow diffident at last,
And care no whit at all,
If spring be come, or the fall be past,
Or how the cool rains fall,

I come to no flower but I pluck,
I raise no cup but I sip,
For a mouth is the best of sweets to suck;
The oldest wine's on the lip.

If I grow old in a year or two,
And come to the querulous song
Of "Alack and aday" and "This was true,
And that, when I was young,"

I must have sweets to remember by,
Some blossom saved from the mire,
Some death-rebellious ember I
Can fan into a fire.

Hunger

(*To Emerson Withorne*)

BREAK me no bread however white it be;
It cannot fill the emptiness I know;
No wine can cool this desert thirst in me
Though it had lain a thousand years in snow;
No swooning lotus flower's languid juice
Drips anodyne unto my restlessness,
And impotent to win me to a truce
Is every artifice of loveliness.
Inevitable is the way I go,
False-faced amid a pageant permeate
With bliss, yet visioning a higher wave
Than this weak ripple washing to and fro;
The fool still keeps his dreams inviolate
Till their virginity espouse the grave.

More Than a Fool's Song

(To Edward Perry)

GO look for beauty where you least
Expect to hear her hive;
Regale your belly with a feast
Of hunger till you thrive.

For honest treatment seek the thief;
For truth consult the liar;
Court pleasure in the halls of grief;
Find smoothness on a briar.

The worth impearled in chastity
Is known best of the harlot,
And courage throws her panoply
On many a native varlet.

In Christian practice those who move
To symbols strange to us
May reckon clearer of His love
Than we who own His cross.

The world's a curious riddle thrown
Water-wise from heaven's cup;
The souls we think are hurtling down
Perhaps are climbing up.

Advice to a Beauty
(*To Sydonia*)

OF all things, lady, be not proud;
Inter not beauty in that shroud
Wherein the living waste, the dead,
Unwept and unrememberéd,
Decay. Beauty beats so frail a wing;
Suffer men to gaze, poets to sing
How radiant you are, compare
And favor you to that most rare
Bird of delight: a lovely face
Matched with an equal inner grace.
Sweet bird, beware the Fowler, Pride;
His knots once neatly crossed and tied,
The prey is caged and walled about
With no way in and no way out.

Ultimatum

I HOLD not with the fatalist creed
Of what must be must be;
There is enough to meet my need
In this most meagre me.

These two slim arms were made to rein
My steed, to ward and fend;
There is more gold in this small brain
Than I can ever spend.

The seed I plant is chosen well;
Ambushed by no sly sweven,
I plant it if it droops to hell,
Or if it blooms to heaven.

At the Wailing Wall in
Jerusalem

OF ALL the grandeur that was Solomon's
High testament of Israel's far pride,
Shedding its lustre like a sun of suns,
This feeble flicker only has not died.
This wall alone reminds a vanquished race,
This brief remembrance still retained in stone,
That sure foundations guard their given place
To rehabilitate the overthrown.

So in the battered temple of the heart,
That grief is harder on than time on stone,
Though three sides crumble, one will stand apart,
Where thought may mourn its past, remembrance groan,
And hands now bare that once were rich with rings
Rebuild upon the ancient site of things.

To Endymion*

ENDYMION, your star is steadfast now,
Beyond aspersion's power to glitter down;
There is no redder blossom on the bough
Of song, no richer jewel in her crown;
Long shall she stammer forth a broken note,
(Striving with how improvident a tongue)
Before the ardor of another throat
Transcends the jubilate you have sung.

High as the star of that last poignant cry
Death could not stifle in the wasted frame,
You know at length the bright immortal lie
Time gives to those detractors of your name,
And see, from where you and Diana ride,
Your humble epitaph—how misapplied!

* Rome, August 1926, after a visit to the grave of Keats.

Epilogue

THE lily, being white not red,
  Contemns the vivid flower,
And men alive believe the dead
  Have lost their vital power.

Yet some prefer the brilliant shade,
  And pass the livid by;
And no man knows if dead men fade
  Or bloom, save those that die.

FROM

THE BLACK CHRIST

———

To the Three for Whom the Book

ONCE like a lady
In a silken dress,
The serpent might eddy
Through the wilderness,
Billow and glow
And undulate
In a rustling flow
Of sinuous hate.
Now dull-eyed and leaden,
Of having lost
His Eden
He pays the cost.
He shuns the tree
That brought him low
As grown to be
Domestic; no
Temptations dapple,
From leaf to root,
The modern apple
Our meekest fruit.
Dragon and griffin
And basilisk
Whose stare could stiffen,
And the hot breath whisk
From the overbold
Braving a gaze
So freezing cold,

Who sings their praise
These latter days?
That venomous head
On a woman fair,—
Medusa's dead
Of the hissing hair.
No beasts are made
Meet for the whir
Of that sunken blade
Excalibur.
No smithies forge
A shining sword
Fit for the gorge
Of a beast abhorred.
Pale Theseus
Would have no need,
Were he with us,
Of sword or thread;
For long has been set
The baleful star
Of Pasiphaë's pet,
The Minotaur.

Though they are dead,
Those ancient ones,
Each bestial head
Dust under tons

Of dust, new beasts
Have come, their heirs,
Claiming their feasts
As the old did theirs.
Clawless they claw,
Fangless they rend;
And the stony maw
Crams on without end.
Still are arrayed
(But with brighter eyes)
Stripling and maid
For the sacrifice.
We cannot spare
This toll we pay
Of the slender, the fair,
The bright and the gay!
Gold and black crown,
Body slim and taut,
How they go down
'Neath the juggernaut!
Youth of the world,
Like scythèd wheat,
How they are hurled
At the clay god's feet!
Hear them cry Holy
To stone and to steel,
See them bend lowly,
Loyal and leal,
Blood rendered and bone,
To steel and to stone.

They have forgot
The stars and the sun,
The grassy plot,
And waters that run
From rock to rock;—
Their only care
Is to grasp a lock
Of Mammon's hair.

But you three rare
Friends whom I love
(With rhymes to swear
The depths whereof)
A book to you three
Who have not bent
The idolatrous knee,
Nor worship lent
To modern rites,
Knowing full well
How a just god smites
The infidel;
Three to whom Pan
Is no mere myth,
But a singing Man
To be reckoned with;—
Witness him now
In the mist and dew;
Lean and hear how
He carols to you:

"Gather as a flower
Living to your heart;
Let the full shower
Rankle and smart;
Youth is the coffer
Where all is hid;
All age may offer
Youth can outbid.
Blind with your beauty
The ranks of scorn,
Take for a duty
Pleasure; you were born
Joy to incur.
Ere the eyes are misted
With a rheumy blur,
Ere the speech is twisted
To a throaty slur,
Ere the cheeks are haggard;
Ere the prick of the spur
Finds you lame or laggard,
Do not demur!
When Time advances
Terrible and lone,
Recall there were dances
Though they be flown.
When Death plys the riddle
To which all are mute,
Remember the fiddle,
The lyre and the flute."

[79]

To three who will heed
His song, nor brook
That a god should plead
In vain, a book.

Tribute
(*To My Mother*)

BECAUSE man is not virtuous in himself,
Nor kind, nor given to sweet charities,
Save goaded by the little kindling elf
Of some dear face it pleasures him to please;
Some men who else were humbled to the dust,
Have marveled that the chastening hand should stay,
And never dreamed they held their lives in trust
To one the victor loved a world away.

So I, least noble of a churlish race,
Least kind of those by nature rough and crude,
Have at the intervention of your face
Spared him with whom was my most bitter feud
One moment, and the next, a deed more grand,
The helpless fly imprisoned in my hand.

That Bright Chimeric Beast

(For Lynn Riggs)

THAT bright chimeric beast
Conceived yet never born,
Save in the poet's breast,
The white-flanked unicorn,
Never may be shaken
From his solitude;
Never may be taken
In any earthly wood.

That bird forever feathered,
Of its new self the sire,
After aeons weathered,
Reincarnate by fire,
Falcon may not nor eagle
Swerve from his eerie,
Nor any crumb inveigle
Down to an earthly tree.

That fish of the dread regime
Invented to become
The fable and the dream
Of the Lord's aquarium,
Leviathan, the jointed
Harpoon was never wrought
By which the Lord's anointed
Will suffer to be caught.

Bird of the deathless breast,
Fish of the frantic fin,
That bright chimeric beast
Flashing the argent skin,—
If beasts like these you'd harry,
Plumb then the poet's dream;
Make it your aviary,

Make it your wood and stream.
There only shall the swish
Be heard of the regal fish;
There like a golden knife
Dart the feet of the unicorn,
And there, death brought to life,
The dead bird be reborn.

Little Sonnet to Little Friends

LET not the proud of heart condemn
Me that I mould my ways to hers,
Groping for healing in a hem
No wind of passion ever stirs;
Nor let them sweetly pity me
When I am out of sound and sight;
They waste their time and energy;
No mares encumber me at night.

Always a trifle fond and strange,
And some have said a bit bizarre,
Say, "Here's the sun," I would not change
It for my dead and burnt-out star.
Shine as it will, I have no doubt
Some day the sun, too, may go out.

Mood

I THINK an impulse stronger than my mind
May some day grasp a knife, unloose a vial,
Or with a little leaden ball unbind
The cords that tie me to the rank and file.
My hands grow quarrelsome with bitterness,
And darkly bent upon the final fray;
Night with its stars upon a grave seems less
Indecent than the too complacent day.

God knows I would be kind, let live, speak fair,
Requite an honest debt with more than just,
And love for Christ's dear sake these shapes that wear
A pride that had its genesis in dust,—
The meek are promised much in a book I know
But one grows weary turning cheek to blow.

Counter Mood

LET this be scattered far and wide, laid low
Upon the waters as they fall and rise,
Be caught and carried by the winds that blow,
Nor let it be arrested by the skies:
I who am mortal say I shall not die;
I who am dust of this am positive,
That though my nights tend toward the grave, yet I
Shall on some brighter day arise, and live.

Ask me not how I am oracular,
Nor whence this arrogant assurance springs.
Ask rather Faith, the canny conjurer,
(Who while your reason mocks him mystifies
Winning the grudging plaudits of your eyes)—
How suddenly the supine egg has wings.

Minutely Hurt

SINCE I was minutely hurt,
Giant griefs and woes
Only find me staunchly girt
Against all other blows.

Once an atom cracks the heart
All is done and said;
Poison, steel, and fiery dart
May then be buffeted.

The Foolish Heart

"BE still, heart, cease those measured strokes;
Lie quiet in your hollow bed;
This moving frame is but a hoax
To make you think you are not dead."

Thus spake I to my body's slave,
With beats still to be answerèd;
Poor foolish heart that needs a grave
To prove to it that it is dead.

For Helen Keller

AGAINST our puny sound and sight
In vain the bells of Heaven ring,
The Mystic Blossoms red and white
May not intrigue our visioning.

For lest we handle, lest we touch,
Lest carnally our minds condone,
Our clumsy credence may not clutch
The under or the overtone.

Her finer alchemy converts
The clanging brass to golden-pealed,
And for her sight the black earth spurts
Hues never thought there unrevealed.

Self Criticism

SHALL I go all my bright days singing,
(A little pallid, a trifle wan)
The failing note still vainly clinging
To the throat of the stricken swan?

Shall I never feel and meet the urge
To bugle out beyond my sense
That the fittest song of earth is a dirge,
And only fools trust Providence?

Than this better the reed never turned flute,
Better than this no song,
Better a stony silence, better a mute
Mouth and a cloven tongue.

A Thorn Forever in the Breast

A HUNGRY cancer will not let him rest
Whose heart is loyal to the least of dreams;
There is a thorn forever in his breast
Who cannot take his world for what it seems;
Aloof and lonely must he ever walk,
Plying a strange and unaccustomed tongue,
An alien to the daily round of talk,
Mute when the sordid songs of earth are sung.

This is the certain end his dream achieves:
He sweats his blood and prayers while others sleep,
And shoulders his own coffin up a steep
Immortal mountain, there to meet his doom
Between two wretched dying men, of whom
One doubts, and one for pity's sake believes.

The Proud Heart

THAT lively organ, palpitant and red,
Enrubied in the staid and sober breast,
Telling the living man, "You are not dead
Until this hammered anvil takes its rest,"
My life's timepiece wound to alarm some day
The body to its need of box and shroud,
Was meant till then to beat one haughty way;
A crimson stroke should be no less than proud.

Yet this high citadel has come to grief
Been broken as an arrow drops its bird,
Splintered as many ways as veins in a leaf
At a woman's laugh or a man's harsh word;
But being proud still strikes its hours in pain;
The dead man lives, and none perceives him slain.

Therefore, Adieu

Now you are gone, and with your unreturning goes
All I had thought in spite of you would stay;
Now draws forever to its unawakening close
The beauty of the bright bandanna'd day.

Now sift in ombrous flakes and revolutions slow
My dreams descending from my heady sky.
The balm I kept to cool my grief in (leaves of snow)
Now melts, with your departure flowing by.

I knew, indeed, the straight unswerving track the sun
Took to your face (as other ecstasies)
Yet I had thought some faith to me in them; they run
From me to you as fly to honey, bees.

Avid, to leave me neither fevered joy nor ache,
Only of soul and body vast unrest.
Sun, moon, and stars should be enough; why must you
     take
The feeling of the heart out of the breast?

Now I who dreamed before I died to shoot one shaft
Of courage from a warped and crooked bow,
Stand utterly forsaken, stripped of that small craft
I had, watching with you all prowess go.

At a Parting

LET us not turn for this aside to die,
Crying a lover may not be a friend.
Our grief is vast enough without that lie;
All stories may not boast a happy end.
Love was a flower, sweet, and flowers fade;
Love was a fairy tale; these have their close.
The endless chronicle was never made,
Nor, save in dreams, the ever-scented rose.

Seeing them dim in passion's diadem,
Our rubies that were bright that now are dull,
Let them not fade without their requiem,
How they were red one time and beautiful,
And how the heart where once a ruby bled
May live, yet bear that mark till it is dead.

Dictum

YEA, I have put thee from me utterly,
And they who plead thy cause do plead in vain;
Window and door are bolted, never key
From any ore shall cozen them again.
This is my regal justice: banishment,
That those who please me now may read and see
How self-sustained I am, with what content
I thrive alike on love or treachery.

God, Thou hast Christ, they say, at Thy right hand;
Close by Thy left Michael is straight and leal;
Around Thy throne the chanting elders stand,
And on the earth Thy feudal millions kneel.
Criest Thou never, Lord, above their song:
"But Lucifer was tall, his wings were long?"

Bright Bindings

YOUR love to me was like an unread book,
Bright-backed, with smooth white pages yet unslit;
Fondly as a lover, foolishly, I took
It from its shelf one day and opened it.
Here shall I read, I thought, beauty and grace,
The soul's most high and awful poetry:—
Alas for lovers and the faith they place
In love, alas for you, alas for me.

I have but read a page or two at most,
The most my horror-blinded eyes may read.
I find here but a windy tapering ghost
Where I sought flesh gifted to ache and bleed.
Yet back you go, though counterfeit you be.
I love bright books even when they fail me.

Ghosts

BREAST under breast when you shall lie
   With him who in my place
Bends over you with flashing eye
   And ever nearing face;

Hand fast in hand when you shall tread
   With him the springing ways
Of love from me inherited
   After my little phase;

Be not surprised if suddenly
   The couch or air confound
Your ravished ears upbraidingly,
   And silence turn to sound.

But never let it trouble you,
   Or cost you one caress;
Ghosts are soon sent with a word or two
   Back to their loneliness.

Song in Spite of Myself

NEVER love with all your heart,
  It only ends in aching;
And bit by bit to the smallest part
  That organ will be breaking.

Never love with all your mind,
  It only ends in fretting;
In musing on sweet joys behind,
  Too poignant for forgetting.

Never love with all your soul,
  For such there is no ending,
Though a mind that frets may find control,
  And a shattered heart find mending.

Give but a grain of the heart's rich seed,
  Confine some under cover,
And when love goes, bid him God-speed.
  And find another lover.

Nothing Endures

NOTHING endures,
Not even love,
Though the warm heart purrs
Of the length thereof.

Though beauty wax,
Yet shall it wane;
Time lays a tax
On the subtlest brain.

Let the blood riot,
Give it its will;
It shall grow quiet,
It shall grow still.

Nirvana gapes
For all things given;
Nothing escapes,
Love not even.

To Certain Critics

THEN call me traitor if you must,
Shout treason and default!
Say I betray a sacred trust
Aching beyond this vault.
I'll bear your censure as your praise,
For never shall the clan
Confine my singing to its ways
Beyond the ways of man.

No racial option narrows grief,
Pain is no patriot,
And sorrow plaits her dismal leaf
For all as lief as not.
With blind sheep groping every hill,
Searching an oriflamme,
How shall the shepherd heart then thrill
To only the darker lamb?

Black Majesty

(After reading John W. Vandercook's chronicle of sable glory)

THESE men were kings, albeit they were black,
Christophe and Dessalines and L'Ouverture;
Their majesty has made me turn my back
Upon a plaint I once shaped to endure.
These men were black, I say, but they were crowned
And purple-clad, however brief their time.
Stifle your agony; let grief be drowned;
We know joy had a day once and a clime.

Dark gutter-snipe, black sprawler-in-the-mud,
A thing men did a man may do again.
What answers filters through your sluggish blood
To these dark ghosts who knew so bright a reign?
"Lo, I am dark, but comely," Sheba sings.
"And we were black," three shades reply, "but kings."

Song of Praise

WHO lies with his milk-white maiden,
Bound in the length of her pale gold hair,
Cooled by her lips with the cold kiss laden,
He lies, but he loves not there.

Who lies with his nut-brown maiden,
Bruised to the bone by her sin-black hair,
Warmed with the wine that her full lips trade in,
He lies, and his love lies there.

Not Sacco and Vanzetti

THESE men who do not die, but send to death,
These iron men whom mercy cannot bend
Beyond the lettered law; what when their breath
Shall suddenly and naturally end?
What shall their final retribution be,
What bloody silver then shall pay the tolls
Exacted for this legal infamy
When death indicts their stark immortal souls?

The day a slumbering but awful God,
Before Time to Eternity is blown,
Examines with the same unyielding rod
These images of His with hearts of stone,
These men who do not die, but death decree,—
These are the men I should not care to be.

handwritten annotation at top: a tale written by a negro Phyllis Wheatly a lady slave — Washington's time

The Black Christ

1

GOD'S glory and my country's shame,
And how one man who cursed Christ's name *[handwritten: gim]*
May never fully expiate
That crime till at the Blessed Gate
Of Heaven He meet *[handwritten: Christ]* and pardon me
Out of His love and charity;
How God, who needs no man's applause,
For love of my stark soul, of flaws
Composed, seeing it slip, did stoop
Down to the mire and pick me up,
And in the hollow of His hand
Enact again at my command
The world's supremest tragedy, *[handwritten: picture of Chris]*
Until I die my burthen be;
How Calvary in Palestine,
Extending down to me and mine,
Was but the first leaf in a line
Of trees on which a Man should swing *[handwritten: Christ hung on cross]*
World without end, in suffering *[handwritten: (Analogy]*
For all men's healing, let me sing. *[handwritten: cross that Christ died & the tree that gim di]*

O world grown indolent and crass,
I stand upon your bleak morass
[handwritten: believe] Of incredulity and cry
Your lack of faith is but a lie.

[104]

If you but brushed the scales apart
That cloud your eyes and clinch your heart
There is no telling what grace might
Be leveled to your clearer sight;
Nor what stupendous choir break
Upon your soul till you should ache
(If you but let your fingers veer,
And raised to heaven a listening ear)
In utter pain in every limb
To know and sing as they that hymn.
If men would set their lips to prayer
With that delight with which they swear,
Heaven and earth as bow and string,
Would meet, would be attuned and sing.

We are diseased, trunk, branch, and shoot;
A sickness gathers at the root
Of us. We flaunt a gaudy fruit
But maggots wrangle at the core.
We cry for angels; yet wherefore,
Who raise no Jacobs any more? . .
No men with eyes quick to perceive
The Shining Thing, clutch at its sleeve,
Against the strength of Heaven try
The valiant force of men who die;—
With heaving heart where courage sings
Strive with a mist of Light and Wings,
And wrestle all night long, though pressed
Be rib to rib and back to breast,

[105]

Till in the end the lofty guest
Pant, "Conquering human, be thou blest."

As once they stood white-plumed and still,
All unobserved on Dothan's hill,
Now, too, the angels, stride for stride,
Would march with us, but are denied.
Did we but let our credence sprout
As we do mockery and doubt,
Lord Christ Himself would stand revealed
In every barren, frosty field
That we misname the heart. Belief
In something more than pain and grief,
In only earth's most commonplace,
Might yet illumine every face
Of wretchedness, each blinded eye,
If from the hermitage where nigh
These thousand years the world of men
Has hemmed her in, might come again
With gracious eyes and gentle breath
The still unconquered Lady, Faith.

Two brothers have I had on earth,
One of spirit, one of sod;
My mother suckled one at birth,
One was the Son of God.

Since that befell which came to me,
Since I was singled out to be,
Upon a wheel of mockery,

The pattern of a new faith spun;
I never doubt that once the sun
For respite stopped in Gibeon,
Or that a Man I could not know
Two thousand ageless years ago,
To shape my profit by His loss,
Bought my redemption on a cross.

2

"Now spring that heals the wounds of earth
Is being born; and in her birth
The wounds of men may find a cure.
By such a thought I may endure,
And of some things be no less sure.
This is a cruel land, this South,
And bitter words to twist my mouth,
Burning my tongue down to its root,
Were quickly found; but I am mute
Before the wonder of this thing:
That God should send so pure a spring,
Such grass to grow, such birds to sing,
And such small trees bravely to sprout
With timid leaves first coming out.
A land spring yearly levies on
Is gifted with God's benison.
The very odor of the loam
Fetters me here to this, my home.
The whitest lady in the town
Yonder trailing a silken gown

[107]

Is less kin to this dirt than I.
Rich mistresses with proud heads high
This dirt and I are one to them;
They flick us both from the bordered hem
Of lovely garments we supply;
But I and the dirt see just as high
As any lady cantering by.
Why should I cut this bond, my son,
This tie too taut to be undone?
This ground and I are we not one?
Has it not birthed and grown and fed me:
Yea, if you will, and also bled me?
That little patch of wizened corn
Aching and straining to be born,
May render back at some small rate
The blood and bone of me it ate.
The weevil there that rends apart
My cotton also tears my heart.
Here too, your father, lean and black,
Paid court to me with all the knack
Of any dandy in the town,
And here were born, and here have grown,
His sons and mine, as lean and black.
What ghosts there are in this old shack
Of births and deaths, soft times and hard!
I count it little being barred
From those who undervalue me.
I have my own soul's ecstasy.
Men may not bind the summer sea,

[108]

Nor set a limit to the stars;
The sun seeps through all iron bars;
The moon is ever manifest.
These things my heart always possessed.
And more than this (and here's the crown)
No man, my son, can batter down
The star-flung ramparts of the mind.
So much for flesh; I am resigned,
Whom God has made shall He not guide?"

So spake my mother, and her pride
For one small minute in its tide
Bore all my bitterness away.
I saw the thin bent form, the gray
Hair shadowed in the candlelight,
The eyes fast parting with their sight,
The rough, brown fingers, lean with toil,
Marking her kinship to the soil.
Year crowding year, after the death
Of that one man whose last drawn breath
Had been the gasping of her name,
She had wrought on, lit with some flame
Her children sensed, but could not see,
And with a patient wizardry
Wheedled her stubborn bit of land
To yield beneath her coaxing hand,
And sometimes in a lavish hour
To blossom even with a flower.
Time after time her eyes grew dim
Watching a life pay for the whim

Some master of the land must feed
To keep her people down. The seed
They planted in her children's breasts
Of hatred toward these men like beasts
She weeded out with legends how
Once there had been somewhere as now *Qwenlites*
A people harried, low in the dust;
But such had been their utter trust
In Heaven and its field of stars
That they had broken down their bars,
And walked across a parted sea
Praising His name who set them free.
I think more than the tales she told,
The music in her voice, the gold
And mellow notes she wrought,
Made us forbear to voice the thought
Low-buried underneath our love,
That we saw things she knew not of.

We had no scales upon our eyes;
God, if He was, kept to His skies,
And left us to our enemies.
Often at night fresh from our knees
And sorely doubted litanies *Rome*
We grappled for the mysteries:
"We never seem to reach nowhere,"
Jim with a puzzled, questioning air,
Would kick the covers back and stare
For me the elder to explain.
As like as not, my sole refrain

Would be, "A man was lynched last night."
"Why?" Jim would ask, his eyes star-bright.
"A white man struck him; he showed fight.
Maybe God thinks such things are right."
"Maybe God never thinks at all—
Of us," and Jim would clench his small,
Hard fingers tight into a ball.

"Likely there ain't no God at all,"
Jim was the first to clothe a doubt
With words, that long had tried to sprout
Against our wills and love of one
Whose faith was like a blazing sun
Set in a dark, rebellious sky.
Now then the roots were fast, and I
Must nurture them in her despite.
God could not be, if He deemed right,
The grief that ever met our sight.

Jim grew; a brooder, silent, sheathed;
But pride was in the air he breathed;
Inside you knew an Ætna seethed.
Often when some new holocaust
Had come to undermine and blast
The life of some poor wretch we knew,
His bones would show like white scars through
His fists in anger's futile way.
"I have a fear," he used to say,
"This thing may come to me some day.

Some man contemptuous of my race
And its lost rights in this hard place,
Will strike me down for being black.
But when I answer I'll pay back
The late revenge long overdue
A thousand of my kind and hue.
A thousand black men, long since gone
Will guide my hand, stiffen the brawn,
And speed one life-divesting blow
Into some granite face of snow.
And I may swing, but not before
I send some pale ambassador
Hot footing it to hell to say
A proud black man is on his way."

When such hot venom curled his lips
And anger snapped like sudden whips
Of lightning in his eyes, her words,—
Slow, gentle as the fall of birds
That having strained to win aloft
Spread out their wings and slowly waft
Regretfully back to the earth,—
Would challenge him to name the worth
Contained in any seed of hate.
Ever the same soft words would mate
Upon her lips: love, trust, and wait.
But he, young, quick, and passionate,
Could not so readily conceal,
Deeper than acid-burns, or steel

Inflicted wounds, his vital hurt;
So still the bitter phrase would spurt:
"The things I've seen, the things I see,
Show what my neighbor thinks of me.
The world is large enough for two
Men any time, of any hue.
I give pale men a wide berth ever;
Best not to meet them, for I never
Could bend my spirit, never truckle
To them; my blood's too hot to knuckle."

And true; the neighbors spoke of him
As that proud nigger, handsome Jim.
It was a grudging compliment,
Half paid in jest, half fair intent,
By those whose partial, jaundiced eye
Saw each of us as one more fly,
Or one more bug the summer brings,
All shaped alike; antennæ, wings,
And noxious all; if caught, to die.
But Jim was not just one more fly,
For he was handsome in a way
Night is after a long, hot day.
If blood flows on from heart to heart,
And strong men leave their counterpart
In vice and virtue in their seed,
Jim's bearing spoke his imperial breed.
I was an offshoot, crude, inclined
More to the earth; he was the kind

Whose every graceful movement said,
As blood must say, by turn of head,
By twist of wrist, and glance of eye,
"Good blood flows here, and it runs high."
He had an ease of limb, a raw,
Clean, hilly stride that women saw
With quickened throbbings of the breast.
There was a show of wings; the nest
Was too confined; Jim needed space
To loop and dip and interlace;
For he had passed the stripling stage,
And stood a man, ripe for the wage
A man extorts of life, his gage
Was down. The beauty of the year
Was on him now, and somewhere near
By in the woods, as like as not,
His cares were laid away, forgot
In hearty wonderment and praise
Of one of spring's all perfect days.

But in my heart a shadow walked
At beauty's side; a terror stalked
For prey this loveliness of time.
A curse lay on this land and clime.
For all my mother's love of it,
Prosperity could not be writ
In any book of destiny
For this most red epitome
Of man's consistent cruelty

[114]

To man. Corruption, blight, and rust
Were its reward, and canker must
Set in. There were too many ghosts
Upon its lanes, too many hosts
Of dangling bodies in the wind,
Too many voices, choked and thinned,
Beseeching mercy on its air.
And like the sea set in my ear
Ever there surged the steady fear
Lest this same end and brutal fate
March toward my proud, importunate
Young brother. Often he'd say,
" 'Twere best, I think, we moved away."
But custom and an unseen hand
Compelled allegiance to this land
In her, and she by staying nailed
Us there, by love securely jailed.

But love and fear must end their bout,
And one or both be counted out.
Rebellion barked now like a gun;
Adam split wide, this faith in one
Who in my sight had never done
One extraordinary thing
That I should praise His name, or sing
His bounty and His grace, let loose
The pent-up torrent of abuse
That clamored in me for release:
"Nay, I have done with deities
Who keep me ever on my knees,

My mouth forever in a tune
Of praise, yet never grant the boon
Of what I pray for night and day.
God is a toy, put Him away.
Or make you one of wood or stone
That you can call your very own,
A thing to feel and touch and stroke,
Who does not break you with a yoke
Of iron that he whispers soft;
Nor promise you fine things aloft
While back and belly here go bare,
While His own image walks so spare
And finds this life so hard to live
You doubt that He has aught to give.
Better an idol shaped of clay
Near you, than one so far away.
Although it may not heed your labors,
At least it will not mind your neighbors'.
'In His own time, He will unfold
You milk and honey, streets of gold,
High walls of jasper . . .' phrases rolled
Upon the tongues of idiots.
What profit *then*, if hunger gluts
Us *now*? Better my God should be
This moving, breathing frame of me,
Strong hands and feet, live heart and eyes;
And when these cease, say then God dies.
Your God is somewhere worlds away
Hunting a star He shot astray;

Oh, He has weightier things to do
Than lavish time on me and you.
What thought has He of us, three motes
Of breath, three scattered notes
In His grand symphony, the world?
Once we were blown, once we were hurled
In place, we were as soon forgot.
He might not linger on one dot
When there were bars and staves to fling
About, for waiting stars to sing.
When Rome was a suckling, when Greece was young,
Then there were Gods fit to be sung,
Who paid the loyal devotee
For service rendered zealously,
In coin a man might feel and spend,
Not marked 'Deferred to Journey's End.'
The servant then was worth his hire;
He went unscathed through flood and fire;
Gods were a thing then to admire.
'Bow down and worship us,' they said.
'You shall be clothed, be housed and fed,
While yet you live, not when you're dead.
Strong are our arms where yours are weak.
On them that harm you will we wreak
The vengeance of a God though they
Were Gods like us in every way.
Not merely is an honor laid
On those we touch with our accolade;
We strike for you with that same blade!' "

[117]

My mother shook a weary head—
"Visions are not for all," she said,
"There were no risings from the dead,
No frightened quiverings of earth
To mark my spirit's latter birth.
The light that on Damascus' road
Blinded a scoffer never glowed
For me. I had no need to view
His side, or pass my fingers through
Christ's wounds. It breaks like that on some,
And yet it can as surely come
Without the lightning and the rain.
Some who must have their hurricane
Go stumbling through it for a light
They never find. Only the night
Of doubt is opened to their sight.
They weigh and measure, search, define,—
But he who seeks a thing divine
Must humbly lay his lore aside,
And like a child believe; confide
In Him whose ways are deep and dark,
And in the end perhaps the spark
He sought will be revealed. Perchance
Some things are hard to countenance,
And others difficult to probe;
But shall the Mind that grew this globe,
And out of chaos thought a world,
To us be totally unfurled?
And all we fail to comprehend,
Shall such a mind be asked to bend

Down to, unravel, and untwine?
If those who highest hold His sign,
Who praise Him most with loudest tongue
Are granted no high place among
The crowd, shall we be bitter then?
The puzzle shall grow simple when
The soul discards the ways of dust.
There is no gain in doubt; but trust
Is our one magic wand. Through it
We and eternity are knit,
Death made a myth, and darkness lit.
The slave can meet the monarch's gaze
With equal pride, dreaming to days
When slave and monarch both shall be,
Transmuted everlastingly,
A single reed blown on to sing
The glory of the only King."

We had not, in the stealthy gloom
Of deepening night, that shot our room
With queerly capering shadows through,
Noticed the form that wavered to
And fro on weak, unsteady feet
Within the door; I turned to greet
Spring's gayest cavalier, but Jim
Who stood there balanced in the dim
Half-light waved me away from him.
And then I saw how terror streaked
His eyes, and how a red flow leaked

And slid from cheek to chin. His hand
Still grasped a knotted branch, and spanned
It fiercely, fondling it. At last
He moved into the light, and cast
His eyes about, as if to wrap
In one soft glance, before the trap
Was sprung, all he saw mirrored there:
All love and bounty; grace; all fair,
All discontented days; sweet weather;
Rain-slant, snow-fall; all things together
Which any man about to die
Might ask to have filmed on his eye,
And then he bowed his haughty head,
"The thing we feared has come," he said;
"But put your ear down to the ground,
And you may hear the deadly sound
Of two-limbed dogs that bay for me.
If any ask in time to be
Why I was parted from my breath,
Here is your tale: I went to death
Because a man murdered the spring.
Tell them though they dispute this thing,
This is the song that dead men sing:
One spark of spirit Godhead gave
To all alike, to sire and slave,
From earth's red core to each white pole,
This one identity of soul;
That when the pipes of beauty play,
The feet must dance, the limbs must sway,

[120]

And even the heart with grief turned lead,
Beauty shall lift like a leaf wind-sped,
Shall swoop upon in gentle might,
Shall toss and tease and leave so light
That never again shall grief or care
Find long or willing lodgement there.
Tell them each law and rule they make
Mankind shall disregard and break
(If this must be) for beauty's sake.
Tell them what pranks the spring can play;
The young colt leaps, the cat that lay
In a sullen ball all winter long
Breaks like a kettle into song;
Waving it high like a limber flail,
The kitten worries his own brief tail;
While man and dog sniff the wind alike,
For the new smell hurts them like a spike
Of steel thrust quickly through the breast;
Earth heaves and groans with a sharp unrest.
The poet, though he sang of death,
Finds tunes for music in simple breath;
Even the old, the sleepy-eyed,
Are stirred to movement by the tide.
But oh, the young, the aging young,
Spring is a sweetmeat to our tongue;
Spring is the pean; we the choir;
Spring is the fuel; we the fire.
Tell them spring's feathery weight will jar,
Though it were iron, any bar

Upreared by men to keep apart
Two who when probed down to the heart
Speak each a common tongue. Tell them
Two met, each stooping to the hem
Of beauty passing by. Such awe
Grew on them hate began to thaw
And fear and dread to melt and run
Like ice laid siege to by the sun.
Say for a moment's misty space
These had forgotten hue and race;
Spring blew too loud and green a blast
For them to think on rank and caste.
The homage they both understood,
(Taught on a bloody Christless rood)
Due from his dark to her brighter blood,
In such an hour, at such a time,
When all their world was one clear rhyme,
He could not give, nor she exact.
This only was a glowing fact:
Spring in a green and golden gown,
And feathered feet, had come to town;
Spring in a rich habiliment
That shook the breath and woke the spent
And sleepy pulse to a dervish beat,
Spring had the world again at her feet.
Spring was a lady fair and rich,
And they were fired with the season's itch
To hold her train or stroke her hair
And tell her shyly they found her fair.

Spring was a voice so high and clear
It broke their hearts as they leaned to hear
In stream and grass and soft bird's-wing;
Spring was in them and they were spring.
Then say, a smudge across the day,
A bit of crass and filthy clay,
A blot of ink upon a white
Page in a book of gold; a tight
Curled worm hid in the festive rose,
A mind so foul it hurt your nose,
Came one of earth's serene elect,
His righteous being warped and flecked
With what his thoughts were: stench and smut. . . .
I had gone on unheeding but
He struck me down, he called her slut,
And black man's mistress, bawdy whore,
And such like names, and many more,—
(Christ, what has spring to answer for!)
I had gone on, I had been wise,
Knowing my value in those eyes
That seared me through and out and in,
Finding a thing to taunt and grin
At in my hair and hue. My right
I knew could not outweigh his might
Who had the law for satellite—
Only I turned to look at her,
The early spring's first worshiper,
  (Spring, what have you to answer for?)
The blood had fled from either cheek
And from her lips; she could not speak,

But she could only stand and stare
And let her pain stab through the air.
I think a blow to heart or head
Had hurt her less than what he said.
A blow can be so quick and kind,
But words will feast upon the mind
And gnaw the heart down to a shred,
And leave you living, yet leave you dead.
If he had only tortured me,
I could have borne it valiantly.
The things he said in littleness
Were cheap, the blow he dealt me less,
Only they totalled more; he gagged
And bound a spirit there; he dragged
A sunlit gown of gold and green,—
(The season's first, first to be seen)
And feathered feet, and a plumèd hat,—
(First of the year to be wondered at)
Through muck and mire, and by the hair
He caught a lady rich and fair.
His vile and puny fingers churned
Our world about that sang and burned
A while as never world before.
He had unlatched an icy door,
And let the winter in once more.
To kill a man is a woeful thing,
But he who lays a hand on spring,
Clutches the first bird by its throat
And throttles it in the midst of a note;

Whose breath upon the leaf-proud tree
Turns all that wealth to penury;
Whose touch upon the first shy flower
Gives it a blight before its hour;
Whose craven face above a pool
That otherwise were clear and cool,
Transforms that running silver dream
Into a hot and sluggish stream
Thus better fit to countenance
His own corrupt unhealthy glance,
Of all men is most infamous;
His deed is rank and blasphemous.
The erstwhile warm, the short time sweet,
Spring now lay frozen at our feet.
Say then, why say nothing more
Except I had to close the door;
And this man's leer loomed in the way.
The air began to sting; then say
There was this branch; I struck; he fell;
There's holiday, I think, in hell."

Outside the night began to groan
As heavy feet crushed twig and stone
Beating a pathway to our door;
A thin noise first, and then a roar
More animal than human grew
Upon the air until we knew
No mercy could be in the sound.
"Quick, hide," I said. I glanced around;
But no abyss gaped in the ground.

[125]

But in the eyes of fear a twig
Will seem a tree, a straw as big
To him who drowns as any raft.
So being mad, being quite daft,
I shoved him in a closet set
Against the wall. This would but let
Him breathe two minutes more, or three,
Before they dragged him out to be
Queer fruit upon some outraged tree.
Our room was in a moment lit
With flaring brands; men crowded it—
Old men whose eyes were better sealed
In sleep; strong men with muscles steeled
Like rods, whose place was in the field;
Striplings like Jim with just a touch
Of down upon the chin; for such
More fitting a secluded hedge
To lie beneath with one to pledge
In youth's hot words, immortal love.
These things they were not thinking of;
"Lynch him! Lynch him!" O savage cry,
Why should you echo, "Crucify!"
One sought, sleek-tongued, to pacify
Them with slow talk of trial, law,
Established court; the dripping maw
Would not be wheedled from its prey.
Out of the past I heard him say,
"So be it then; have then your way;
But not by me shall blood be spilt;
I wash my hands clean of this guilt."

[126]

This was an echo of a phrase
Uttered how many million days
Gone by?
        Water may cleanse the hands
But what shall scour the soul that stands
Accused in heaven's sight?
                "The Kid."
One cried, "Where is the bastard hid?"
"He is not here."
                It was a faint
And futile lie.
            "The hell he ain't;
We tracked him here. Show us the place,
Or else . . . ."
                He made an ugly face,
Raising a heavy club to smite.
I had been felled, had not the sight
Of all been otherwise arraigned.
Each with bewilderment unfeigned
Stared hard to see against the wall
The hunted boy stand slim and tall;
Dream-born, it seemed, with just a trace
Of weariness upon his face,
He stood as if evolved from air;
As if always he had stood there. . . .
What blew the torches' feeble flare
To such a soaring fury now?
Each hand went up to fend each brow,
Save his; he and the light were one,
A man by night clad with the sun.

[127]

By form and feature, bearing, name,
I knew this man. He was the same
Whom I had thrust, a minute past,
Behind a door,—and made it fast.
Knit flesh and bone, had like a thong,
Bound us as one our whole life long,
But in the presence of this throng,
He seemed one I had never known.
Never such tragic beauty shone
As this on any face before.
It pared the heart straight to the core.
It is the lustre dying lends,
I thought, to make some brief amends
To life so wantonly cut down.
The air about him shaped a crown
Of light, or so it seemed to me,
And sweeter than the melody
Of leaves in rain, and far more sad,
His voice descended on the mad,
Blood-sniffing crowd that sought his life,
A voice where grief cut like a knife:
"I am he whom you seek, he whom
You will not spare his daily doom.
My march is ever to the tomb,
But let the innocent go free;
This man and woman, let them be,
Who loving much have succored me."
And then he turned about to speak
To me whose heart was fit to break,

"My brother, when this wound has healed,
And you reap in some other field
Roses, and all a spring can yield;
Brother (to call me so!) then prove
Out of your charity and love
That I was not unduly slain,
That this my death was not in vain.
For no life should go to the tomb
Unless from it a new life bloom,
A greater faith, a clearer sight,
A wiser groping for the light."
He moved to where our mother stood,
Dry-eyed, though grief was at its flood, *he speaks to mother*
"Mother, not poorer losing one,
Look now upon your dying son."
Her own life trembling on the brim,
She raised woe-ravaged eyes to him,
And in their glances something grew
And spread, till healing fluttered through
Her pain, a vision so complete
It sent her humbly to his feet
With what I deemed a curious cry,
"And must this be for such as I?"
Even his captors seemed to feel
Disquietude, an unrest steal
Upon their ardor, dampening it,
Till one less fearful varlet hit
Him across the mouth a heavy blow,
Drawing a thin, yet steady flow
Of red to drip a dirge of slow

[129]

Finality upon my heart.
The end came fast. Given the start
One hound must always give the pack
That fears the meekest prey whose back
Is desperate against a wall,
They charged. I saw him stagger, fall
Beneath a mill of hands, feet, staves.
And I like one who sees huge waves
In hunger rise above the skiff
At sea, yet watching from a cliff
Far off can lend no feeblest aid,
No more than can a fragile blade
Of grass in some far distant land,
That has no heart to wrench, nor hand
To stretch in vain, could only stand
With streaming eyes and watch the play.
There grew a tree a little way
Off from the hut, a virgin tree
Awaiting its fecundity.

O Tree was ever worthier Groom
Led to a bride of such rare bloom?
Did ever fiercer hands enlace
Love and Beloved in an embrace
As heaven-smiled-upon as this?
Was ever more celestial kiss?
But once, did ever anywhere
So full a choir chant such an air
As feathered splendors bugled there?
And was there ever blinder eye
Or deafer ear than mine?

suggest
immaculate
concept

A cry

So soft, and yet so brimming filled
With agony, my heart strings thrilled
An ineffectual reply,—
Then gaunt against the southern sky
The silent handiwork of hate.
Greet, Virgin Tree, your holy mate!

No sound then in the little room
Was filtered through my sieve of gloom,
Except the steady fall of tears,
The hot, insistent rain that sears
The burning ruts down which it goes,
The futile flow, for all one knows
How vain it is, that ever flows.
I could not bear to look at *her*
There in the dark; I could not stir
From where I sat, so weighted down.
The king of grief, I held my crown
So dear, I wore my tattered gown
With such affection and such love
That though I strove I could not move.
But I could hear (and this unchained
The raging beast in me) her pained
And sorrow-riven voice ring out
Above the spirit's awful rout,
Above the howling winds of doubt,
How she knew Whom she traveled to
Was judge of all that men might do

To such as she who trusted Him.
Faith was a tower for her, grim
And insurmountable; and death
She said was only changing breath
Into an essence fine and rare.
Anger smote me and most despair
Seeing her still bow down in prayer.
"Call on Him now," I mocked, "and try
Your faith against His deed, while I
With intent equally as sane,
Searching a motive for this pain,
Will hold a little stone on high
And seek of it the reason why.
Which, stone or God, will first reply?
Why? Hear me ask it. He was young
And beautiful. Why was he flung
Like common dirt to death? Why, stone,
Must he of all the earth atone
For what? The dirt God used was homely
But the man He made was comely.
What child creating out of sand,
With puckered brow and intent hand,
Would see the lovely thing he planned
Struck with a lewd and wanton blade,
Nor stretch a hand to what he made,
Nor shed a childish, futile tear,
Because he loved it, held it dear?
Would not a child's weak heart rebel?
But Christ who conquered Death and Hell

What has He done for you who spent
A bleeding life for His content?
Or is the white Christ, too, distraught
By these dark sins His Father wrought?"

I mocked her so until I broke
Beneath my passion's heavy yoke.
My world went black with grief and pain;
My very bitterness was slain,
And I had need of only sleep,
Or some dim place where I might weep
My life away, some misty haunt
Where never man might come to taunt
Me with the thought of how men scar
Their brothers here, or what we are
Upon this most accursèd star.
Not that sweet sleep from which some wake
All fetterless, without an ache
Of heart or limb, but such a sleep
As had raped him, eternal, deep;—
Deep as my woe, vast as my pain,
Sleep of the young and early-slain.
My Lycidas was dead. There swung
In all his glory, lusty, young,
My Jonathan, my Patrocles,
(For with his death there perished these)
And I had neither sword nor song,
Only an acid-bitten tongue,
Fit neither in its poverty

[133]

For vengeance nor for threnody,
Only for tears and blasphemy.

Now God be praised that a door should creak,
And that a rusty hinge should shriek.
Of all sweet sounds that I may hear
Of lute or lyre or dulcimer,
None ever shall assail my ear
Sweet as the sound of a grating door
I had thought closed forevermore.
Out of my deep-ploughed agony,
I turned to see a door swing free;
The very door he once came through
To death, now framed for us anew
His vital self, his and no other's
Live body of the dead, my brother's.
Like one who dreams within a dream,
Hand at my throat, lest I should scream,
I moved with hopeful, doubting pace
To meet the dead man face to face.

"Bear witness now unto His grace";
I heard my mother's mounting word,
"Behold the glory of the Lord,
His unimpeachable high seal.
Cry mercy now before Him; kneel,
And let your heart's conversion swell
The wonder of His miracle."

I saw; I touched; yet doubted him;
My fingers faltered down his slim

Sides, down his breathing length of limb.
Incredulous of sight and touch,
"No more," I cried, "this is too much
For one mad brain to stagger through."
For there he stood in utmost view
Whose death I had been witness to;
But now he breathed; he lived; he walked;
His tongue could speak my name; he talked.
He questioned me to know what art
Had made his enemies depart.
Either I leaped or crawled to where
I last had seen stiff on the air
The form than life more dear to me;
But where had swayed that misery
Now only was a flowering tree
That soon would travail into fruit.
Slowly my mind released its mute
Bewilderment, while truth took root
In me and blossomed into light:
"Down, down," I cried, in joy and fright,
As all He said came back to me
With what its true import must be,
"Upon our knees and let the worst,
Let me the sinfullest kneel first;
O lovely Head to dust brought low
More times than we can ever know
Whose small regard, dust-ridden eye,
Behold Your doom, yet doubt You die;
O Form immaculately born,
Betrayed a thousand times each morn,

[135]

As many times each night denied,
Surrendered, tortured, crucified!
Now have we seen beyond degree
That love which has no boundary;
Our eyes have looked on Calvary."

No sound then in the sacred gloom
That blessed the shrine that was our room
Except the steady rise of praise
To Him who shapes all nights and days
Into one final burst of sun;
Though with the praise some tears must run
In pity of the King's dear breath
That ransomed one of us from death.

The days are mellow for us now;
We reap full fields; the heavy bough
Bends to us in another land;
The ripe fruit falls into our hand.
My mother, Job's dark sister, sits
Now in a corner, prays, and knits.
Often across her face there flits
Remembered pain, to mar her joy,
At Whose death gave her back her boy.
While I who mouthed my blasphemies,
Recalling now His agonies,
Am found forever on my knees,
Ever to praise her Christ with her,
Knowing He can at will confer

Magic on miracle to prove
And try me when I doubt His love.
If I am blind He does not see;
If I am lame He halts with me;
There is no hood of pain I wear
That has not rested on His hair
Making Him first initiate
Beneath its harsh and hairy weight.
He grew with me within the womb;
He will receive me at the tomb.
He will make plain the misty path
He makes me tread in love and wrath,
And bending down in peace and grace
May wear again my brother's face.
Somewhere the Southland rears a tree,
 (And many others there may be
Like unto it, that are unknown,
Whereon as costly fruit has grown).
It stands before a hut of wood
In which the Christ Himself once stood—
And those who pass it by may see
Nought growing there except a tree,
But there are two to testify
Who hung on it . . . we saw Him die.
Its roots were fed with priceless blood.
It is the Cross; it is the Rood. *Cross*

Paris, January 31, 1929

*Christ was crucified on a
dogwood tree.*

FROM

THE MEDEA

———

After a Visit

(At Padraic Colum's where there were Irish poets)

LAST night I lay upon my bed and would have slept;
But all around my head was wet with tears I wept,
As bitter dreams swarmed in like bees to sting my brain,
While others kissed like endless snakes forged in a
    chain,
Dull-eyed Euminedes estranging me and sleep,
Each soft insidious caress biting me deep.
And I wept not what I had done but what let go,
Between two seasons, one of fire and one of snow.
I had known joy and sorrow I had surely known,
But out of neither any piercing note was blown.
Friends had been kind and surely friends had faithless
    been,
But long ago my heart was closed, panelled within.
And I had walked two seasons through, and moved among
Strange ways and folk, and all the while no line was
    wrung
In praise or blame of aught from my frost-bitten tongue.
Silence had sunned me with her hot, embalming mouth,
And indolence had watered me with drops of drouth.
Then I walked in a room where Irish poets were;
I saw the muse enthroned, heard how they worshiped her,
Felt men nor gods could ever so envenom them
That Poetry could pass and they not grasp her hem,
Not cry on her for healing; shaken off, still praise,
Not questioning her enigmatical delays.

And shame of my apostasy was like a coal
That reached my tongue and heart and far off frigid soul,
Melting myself into myself, making me weep
Regeneration's burning tears, preluding sleep.

Magnets

THE straight, the swift, the debonair,
Are targets on the thoroughfare
For every kind appraising eye;
Sweet words are said as they pass by.
But such a strange contrary thing
My heart is, it will never cling
To any bright unblemished thing.
Such have their own security,
And little need to lean on me.
The limb that falters in its course,
And cries, "Not yet!" to waning force;
The orb that may not brave the sun;
The bitter mouth, its kissing done;
The loving heart that must deny
The very love it travels by;
What most has need to bend and pray,
These magnets draw my heart their way.

Any Human to Another

THE ills I sorrow at
Not me alone
Like an arrow,
Pierce to the marrow,
Through the fat
And past the bone.

Your grief and mine
Must intertwine
Like sea and river,
Be fused and mingle,
Diverse yet single,
Forever and forever.

Let no man be so proud
And confident,
To think he is allowed
A little tent
Pitched in a meadow
Of sun and shadow
All his little own.

Joy may be shy, unique,
Friendly to a few,
Sorrow never scorned to speak
To any who
Were false or true.

Your every grief
Like a blade
Shining and unsheathed
Must strike me down.
Of bitter aloes wreathed,
My sorrow must be laid
On your head like a crown.

Only the Polished Skeleton

THE heart has need of some deceit
 To make its pistons rise and fall;
For less than this it would not beat,
 Nor flush the sluggish vein at all.

With subterfuge and fraud the mind
 Must fend and parry thrust for thrust,
With logic brutal and unkind
 Beat off the onslaughts of the dust.

Only the polished skeleton,
 Of flesh relieved and pauperized,
Can rest at ease and think upon
 The worth of all it so despised.

To France

THOUGH I am not the first in English terms
To name you of the earth's great nations Queen;
Though better poets chant it to the worms
How that fair city perched upon the Seine
Is lovelier than that they traveled to;
While kings and warriors and many a priest
In their last hour have smiled to think of you,
Among these count me not the last nor least.

As he whose eyes are gouged craves light to see,
And he whose limbs are broken strength to run,
So have I sought in you that alchemy
That knits my bones and turns me to the sun;
And found across a continent of foam
What was denied my hungry heart at home.

Medusa

I MIND me how when first I looked at her
A warning shudder in the blood cried, "Ware!
Those eyes are basilisk's she gazes through,
And those are snakes you take for strands of hair!"
But I was never one to be subdued
By any fear of aught not reason-bred,
And so I mocked the ruddy word, and stood
To meet the gold-envenomed dart instead.

O vengeful warning, spiteful stream, a truce!
What boots this constant crying in the wind,
This ultimate indignity: abuse
Heaped on a tree of all its foliage thinned?
Though blind, yet on these arid balls engraved
I know it was a lovely face I braved.

Sonnet

I HAVE not loved you in the noblest way
The human heart can beat, where what it loves
Is canonized and purged, outtops the day
To masquerade beneath itself,—as gloves
Upon a pilfering hand (sly fingers) laid,
Can make them move as something frank and kind,—
Yet in the curved-up palm is niched a blade;
Loved have I much, but I have not been blind.

The noblest way is fraught with too much pain;
Who travels it must drag a crucifix;
What hurts my heart hurts deep and to the grain;
My mother never dipped me in the Styx,
And who would find me weak and vulnerable
Need never aim his arrow at my heel.

Sonnet

SOME for a little while do love, and some for long;
And some rare few forever and for aye;
Some for the measure of a poet's song,
And some the ribbon width of a summer's day.
Some on a golden crucifix do swear,
And some in blood do plight a fickle troth;
Some struck divinely mad may only stare,
And out of silence weave an iron oath.

So many ways love has none may appear
The bitter best, and none the sweetest worst;
Strange food the hungry have been known to bear,
And brackish water slakes an utter thirst.
It is a rare and tantalizing fruit
Our hands reach for, but nothing absolute.

Sonnet

I KNOW now how a man whose blood is hot
And rich, still undiminished of desire,
Thinking (too soon), "The world is dust and mire,"
Must feel who takes to wife four walls, a cot,
A hempen robe and cowl, saying, "I'll not
To anything, save God and Heaven's fire,
Permit a thought; and I will never tire
Of Christ, and in Him all shall be forgot."

He too, as it were Torquemada's rack,
Writhes piteously on that unyielding bed,
Crying, "Take Heaven all, but give me back
Those words and sighs without which I am dead;
Which thinking on are lances, and I reel."
Letting you go, I know how he would feel.

To One Not There

(For D. W.)

THIS is a land in which you never were,
A land perchance which you may never see;
And yet the length of it I may not stir,
But your sweet spirit walks its ways with me.
Your voice is in these Gallic accents light,
And sweeter is the Rhenish wine I sip
Because this glass (a lesser Grail) is bright
Illumined by the memory of your lip.

Thus would I have it in the dismal day,
When I fare forth upon another ship,
The heart not warm as now; but cold, and clay;
The journey forced; not, sweet, a pleasure trip.
Thus would I take your image by the hand,
But leave you safe within a living land.

Paris, July 1933

Sonnet

WHAT I am saying now was said before,
And countless centuries from now again,
Some poet warped with bitterness and pain,
Will brew like words hoping to salve his sore.
And seeing written he will think the core
Of anguish from that throbbing wound, his brain,
Squeezed out; and these ill humours gone, disdain,
Or think he does, the face he loved of yore.

And then he too, as I, will turn to look
Upon his instrument of discontent,
Thinking himself a Perseus, and fit to brook
Her columned throat and every blandishment;
And looking know what brittle arms we wield,
Whose pencil is our sword, whose page our shield.

Sonnet

THESE are no wind-blown rumors, soft say-sos,
No garden-whispered hearsays, lightly heard
I know that summer never spares the rose,
That spring is faithless to the brightest bird.
I know that nothing lovely shall prevail
To win from Time and Death a moment's grace;
At Beauty's birth the scythe was honed, the nail
Dipped for her hands, the cowl clipped for her face.

And yet I cannot think that this my faith,
My wingèd joy, my pride, my utmost mirth,
Centered in you, shall ever taste of death,
Or perish from the false, forgetting earth.
You are with time, as wind and weather are,
As is the sun, and every nailèd star.

Sonnet Dialogue

I to My Soul:

Why this preoccupation, soul, with Death,
This servile genuflexion to the worm,
Making the tomb a Mecca where the breath
(Though still it rises vaporous, but firm,
Expelled from lungs still clear and unimpaired,
To plough through nostrils quivering with pride)
Veers in distress and love, as if it dared
Not search a gayer place, and there subside?

My Soul to Me:

Because the worm shall tread the lion down,
And in the end shall sicken at its feast,
And for a worm of even less renown
Loom as a dread but subjugated beast;
Because whatever lives is granted breath
But by the grace and sufferance of Death.

To France

I have a dream of where (when I grow old,
Having no further joy to take in lip
Or limb, a graybeard caching from the cold
The frail indignity of age) some ship
Might bear my creaking, unhinged bones
Trailing remembrance as a tattered cloak,
And beach me glad, though on their sharpest stones,
Among a fair and kindly foreign folk.

There might I only breathe my latest days,
With those rich accents falling on my ear
That most have made me feel that freedom's rays
Still have a shrine where they may leap and sear,—
Though I were palsied there, or halt, or blind,
So I were there, I think I should not mind.

Death to the Poor

(From the French of Baudelaire)

IN death alone is what consoles; and life
And all its end is death; and that fond hope
Whose music like a mad fantastic fife
Compels us up this ridged and rocky slope.
Through lightning, hail, and hurt of human look,
Death is the vibrant light we travel toward,
The mystic Inn forepromised in the Book
Where all are welcomed in to bed and board.

An angel whose star-banded fingers hold
The gift of dreams and calm, ecstatic sleep
In easier beds than those we had before,
Death is the face of God, the only fold
That pens content and ever-happy sheep,
To Paradise the only open door.

The Cat

(From the French of Baudelaire)

COME, lovely cat, to this adoring breast;
Over thy daggers silken scabbards draw;
Into thy beauty let me plunge to rest,
Unmindful of thy swift and cruel claw.
The while my fingers leisurely caress
Thy head and vaulted back's elastic arch,
And through each tip mysterious pleasures press
And crackle on their swift dynamic march,
I see revived in thee, felinely cast,
A woman with thine eyes, satanic beast,
Profound and cold as scythes to mow me down.
And from her feet up to her throat are massed
Strange aromas; a perfume from the East
Swims round her body, sinuous and brown.

Cats

(From the French of Baudelaire)

LOVERS that burn and learnèd scholars cold
Dote equally in their appointed time
On subtle cats which do them both combine—
Quiet as scholars and as lovers bold.
Friendly alike to sage and sybarite,
They thrive on silence; shadow is their friend;
Earth's fittest runners for the Prine of Night,
Unto no other pride their own will bend.

In noble attitudes they sit and dream,
Small sphinxes miming those in lonelier lands,
In stony sleep eternal and afar.
With passion's seed their fruitful bodies teem,
While golden scintilla like burning sands
Their eyes with mystery and light bestar.

Scottsboro, Too, Is Worth Its Song

(A poem to American poets)

I SAID:
Now will the poets sing,—
Their cries go thundering
Like blood and tears
Into the nation's ears,
Like lightning dart
Into the nation's heart.
Against disease and death and all things fell,
And war,
Their strophes rise and swell
To jar
The foe smug in his citadel.

Remembering their sharp and pretty
Tunes for Sacco and Vanzetti,
I said:
Here too's a cause divinely spun
For those whose eyes are on the sun,
Here in epitome
Is all disgrace
And epic wrong,
Like wine to brace
The minstrel heart, and blare it into song.

Surely, I said,
Now will the poets sing.
But they have raised no cry.
I wonder why.

UNPUBLISHED POEMS

Dear Friends and Gentle Hearts *

WE open infant eyes
Of wonder and surprise
Upon a world all strange and new,
Too vast to please our childish view,
Yet love bends down and trust imparts;
We gaze around
And know we've found
Dear friends and gentle hearts;
Good-day, we smile, dear friends and gentle hearts;
Good-day dear friends and gentle hearts.

When on the western rim
Of time the sun grows dim,
And dimly on the closing eye
Fadeth the earth, the sea, the sky,
How blessedly this breath departs
If it pass out
While watch about
Dear friends and gentle hearts;
Good-night, we smile, dear friends and gentle hearts;
Good-night, dear friends, and gentle hearts.

April 1943

Lines for a Hospital

YE blind, ye deaf, ye mute! Ho, here's healing!
 Here's light to brim
 The eyeball dim;
 Here's sound to cheer
 The muted ear;
 Ways to oppose
 The wayward nose,
 And make sweet notes
 From locked throats
Like chimes cascading come, all pealing:
 Ho, here's healing.

November 1943

A Negro Mother's Lullaby
(*After visiting John Brown's grave*)

HUSHABY, hushaby, dark one at my knee;
Slumber you softly, nor pucker, nor frown;
Though some may be bonded, you shall be free,
Thanks to a man . . . Osawatamie Brown.
    His sons are high fellows,
    An Archangel is he,
    And they doff their bright haloes
    To none but the Three.

Hushaby, hushaby, sweet darkness at rest,
Two there have been who their lives laid down
That you might be beautiful here at my breast:
Our Jesus and . . . Osawatamie Brown.
    His sons are high fellows,
    An Archangel is he,
    And they doff their bright haloes
    To none but the Three.

Hushaby, hushaby, when a man, not a slave,
    With freedom for wings you go through the town,
Let your love be dew on his evergreen grave;
Sleep, in the name of Osawatamie Brown.
    Rich counsel he's giving
    Close by the throne,
    Tall he was living
    But now taller grown.

His sons are high fellows,
An Archangel is he,
And they doff their bright haloes
To none but the Three.

Lake Placid, N. Y.
August 1941

Karenge ya Marenge*

WHEREIN are words sublime or noble? What
Invests one speech with haloed eminence,
Makes it the sesame for all doors shut,
Yet in its like sees but impertinence?
Is it the hue? Is it the cast of eye,
The curve of lip or Asiatic breath,
Which mark a lesser place for Gandhi's cry
Than "Give me liberty or give me death!"

Is Indian speech so quaint, so weak, so rude,
So like its land enslaved, denied, and crude,
That men who claim they fight for liberty
Can hear this battle-shout impassively,
Yet to their arms with high resolve have sprung
At those same words cried in the English tongue?

August 19, 1942

* Do or die. . . . Gandhi

Christus Natus Est

IN Bethlehem
On Christmas morn,
The lowly gem
Of love was born.
Hosannah! *Christus natus est.*

Bright in her crown
Of fiery star,
Judea's town
Shone from afar:
Hosannah! *Christus natus est.*

While beasts in stall,
On bended knee,
Did carol all
Most joyously:
Hosannah! *Christus natus est.*

For bird and beast
He did not come,
But for the least
Of mortal scum.
Hosannah! *Christus natus est.*

Who lies in ditch?
Who begs his bread?

Who has no stitch
For back or head?
Hosannah! *Christus natus est.*

Who wakes to weep,
Lies down to mourn?
Who in his sleep
Withdraws from scorn?
Hosannah! *Christus natus est.*

Ye outraged dust,
On field and plain,
To feed the lust
Of madmen slain:
Hosannah! *Christus natus est.*

The manger still
Outshines the throne;
Christ must and will
Come to his own.
Hosannah! *Christus natus est.*

Christmas 1943

La Belle, La Douce, La Grande

FRANCE! How shall we call her belle again?
Does loveliness reside
In sunken cheeks, in bellies barren and denied?
What twisted inconsistent pen
Can ever call her belle again?
Or douce? Can gentleness invade
The frozen heart, the mind betrayed,
Or search for refuge in the viper's den?
How shall we call her douce again?
Or grande? Did greatness ever season
The broth of shame, repudiation, treason?
Or shine upon the lips of little lying men?
How shall we call her grande again?

Has history no memory, nor reason?
What land inhabited of men
Has never known that dark hour when
First it felt the sting of treason?
Petain? Laval? Can they outweigh
By an eyelash or a stone
The softest word she had to say,
That sainted soul of France called Joan?

Nay even now, look up, see fall
As on Elisha Elijah's shawl,
Joan's mantle on the gaunt De Gaulle:

New Knight of France, great paladin,
Behold him sally forth to win
Her place anew at freedom's hand,
A place for France: la belle, la douce, la grande.

July 10, 1944

THE BALLAD OF THE BROWN GIRL

AN OLD BALLAD RETOLD
(To Witter Bynner)

———

The Ballad of the Brown Girl

OH, this is the tale the grandams tell
In the land where the grass is blue,
And some there are who say 'tis false,
And some that hold it true.

. . . .

Lord Thomas on a summer's day
Came to his mother's door;
His eyes were ringed for want of sleep;
His heart was troubled sore.

He knelt him at his mother's side;
She stroked his curly head.
"I've come to be advised of you;
Advise me well," he said.

"For there are two who love me well—
I wot it from each mouth—
And one's Fair London, lily maid,
And pride of all the south.

She is full shy and sweet as still
Delight when nothing stirs;
My soul can thrive on love of her,
And all my heart is hers."

His mother's slender fingers ploughed
Dark furrows through his hair,

[175]

"The other one who loves you well,
Is she as sweet and fair?"

"She is the dark Brown Girl who knows
No more-defining name,
And bitter tongues have worn their tips
In sneering at her shame."

"But there are lands to go with her,
And gold and silver stores."
His mother whispered in his ear,
"And all her heart is yours."

His mother loved the clink of gold,
The odor and the shine
Of larders bowed with venison
And crystal globes of wine.

"Oh, love is good," the lady quoth,
"When berries ripe and sweet,
From every bush and weighted vine
Are crying, 'Take and eat.' "

"But what is best when winter comes
Is gold and silver bright;
Go bring me home the nut-brown maid
And leave the lily-white."

He sent his criers through the land
To cry his wedding day,
But bade them at Fair London's road
To turn the other way.

His bridal day dawned white and fair,
His heart held night within;
He heard its anguished beats above
The jocund wedding din.

The Brown Girl came to him as might
A queen to take her crown;
With gems her fingers flamed and flared;
Her robe was weighted down.

Her hair was black as sin is black
And ringed about with fire;
Her eyes were black as night is black
When moon and stars conspire;
Her mouth was one red cherry clipt
In twain, her voice a lyre.

Lord Thomas took her jewelled hand,
The holy words were said,
And they have made the holy vow
To share one board and bed.

But suddenly the furious feast
Is shattered with a shout;
Lord Thomas trembles at the word,
"Fair London is without."

All pale and proud she stands without,
And will not venture in;
He leaves the side of his nut-brown bride
To bid her enter in.

Her skin was white as almond milk
Slow trickling from the flower;
Her frost-blue eyes were darkening
Like clouds before a shower;

Her thin pink lips were twin rosebuds
That had not come to flower,
And crowning all, her golden hair
Was loosened out in shower.

He has taken her by her slim white hand,
(Oh, light was her hand in his)
But the touch ran wild and fierce and hot,
And burned like a brand in his.

"Lord Thomas," she said; her voice was low,
"I come unbidden here,
But I have come to see your bride
And taste your bridal cheer."

He has taken her by her slim white hand
And led her to his bride,
And brown and white have bent them low,
And sat them side by side.

He has brimmed a cup with the wedding wine,
He has placed it in her hand,
She has raised it high and smiled on him
Like love in a distant land.

"I came to see your bonny bride,
I came to wish you well,"

Her voice was clear as song is clear;
Clear as a silver bell.

"But, Thomas, Lord, is this your bride?
I think she's mighty brown;
Why didn't you marry a fair, bright girl
As ever the sun shone on?

For only the rose and the rose should mate,
Oh, never the hare and the hound,"
And the wine he poured for her crimson mouth
She poured upon the ground.

The flow of wine and jest has ceased,
The groom has flushed and paled,
The Brown Girl's lips are moist and red
Where her sharp white teeth assailed.

Dark wrath has climbed her nut-brown throat,
And wrath in her wild blood sings,
But she tramples her passions underfoot
Because she comes of kings.

She has taken her stand by her rival's side,
"Lord Thomas, you have heard,
As I am yours and you are mine
By ring and plighted word,
Avenge me here on our bridal day."—
Lord Thomas spoke no word.

The Brown Girl's locks were held in place
By a dagger serpentine;

Thin it was and long and sharp,
And tempered well and fine.

And legend claimed that a dusky queen,
In a dusky dream-lit land,
Had loved in vain, and died of it,
By her own slim twilight hand.

The Brown Girl's hair has kissed her waist,
Her hand has closed on steel;
Fair London's blood has joined the wine
She sullied with her heel.

Lord Thomas caught her as she fell,
And cried, "My sweet, my fair,
Dark night has hid the golden sun,
And blood has thicked the air.

The little hand that should have worn
A golden band for me,
The little hand that fluttered so
Is still as death can be."

He bent and kissed the weeping wound
Fresh in her heart's young core,
And then he kissed her sleeping mouth
That would not waken more.

He seized the Brown Girl's rippling hair
That swung in eddies loose,
And with one circle of his arm
He made a hairy noose.

He pulled it till she swooned for pain,
And spat a crimson lake;
He pulled it till a something snapped
That was not made to break.

And her he loved he brought and placed
By her who was his bride,
And brown and white like broken buds
Kept vigil side by side.

And one was like a white, white rose
Whose inmost heart has bled,
And one was like a red, red rose
Whose roots have witherèd.

Lord Thomas took a golden harp
That hung above his head;
He picked its strings and played a tune
And sang it to the dead.

"O lovers never barter love
For gold or fertile lands,
For love is meat and love is drink,
And love heeds love's commands."

"And love is shelter from the rain,
And scowling stormy skies;
Who casts off love must break his heart,
And rue it till he dies."

And then he hugged himself and grinned,
And laughed, "Ha, ha," for glee;

But those who watched knew he was mad,
And shudderèd to see.

And some made shift to go to him,
But there was in his eye
What made each man to turn aside
To let his neighbor by.

His mother in a satin gown
Was fain to go to him,
But his lips curled back like a gray wolf's fang,
When the huntsmen blow to him.

"No mother of mine, for gold's the god
Before whose feet you fall;
Here be two dead who will be three,
And you have slain us all.

Go dig one grave to hold us all
And make it deep and wide;
And lay the Brown Girl at my feet,
Fair London by my side."

And as he spoke his hand went up,
And singing steel swept down,
And as its kiss betrayed his heart,
Death wore a triple crown.

And in the land where the grass is blue,
In a grave dug deep and wide,
The Brown Girl sleeps at her true lord's feet,
Fair London by his side.

The Wakeupworld

THIS was the song of the Wakeupworld,
The beautiful beast with long tail curled:

"Wake up, O World; O World, awake!
The light is bright on hill and lake;
O World, awake; wake up, O World!
The flags of the wind are all unfurled;
Wake up, O World; O World, awake!
Of earth's delightfulness partake.

Wake up, O World, whatever hour;
Sweet are the fields, sweet is the flower!
Wake up, O World; O World, awake;
Perhaps to see the daylight break,
Perhaps to see the sun descend,
The night begin, the daylight end.

But something surely to behold,
Not bought with silver or with gold,
Not shown in any land of dreams.
For open eyes the whole world teems
With lovely things to do or make,
Wake up, O World; O World, awake!"

Such was the song of the Wakeupworld,
The beautiful beast with long tail curled,
The Wakeupworld so swift and fleet,
With twelve bright eyes and six strong feet.

Such was the song he sang all day,
Lest man or beast should sleep away
The gift of Time, and never know
The beauties of this life below.
Twelve were his eyes, as I have said,
Placed clockwise in his massive head.
Never in any time or weather
Were all those eyes shut tight together,
But daily, at its certain hour,
Each eye became possessed of power.

At one, an eye all pale and white
Flew open for the day's first sight,
And looked alone, until at two
There woke his wondering eye of blue.
His eye of green at stroke of three
Blazed like a jewel brilliantly;
At four he opened up the red,
And all around its lustre spread.
Shyly then, as if all sleepy yet,
At five peeped forth the violet.
An eye of silver, chill and cold,
The hour of six would then unfold.
At seven with a sudden wink,
He would let loose his eye of pink.
At eight an eye so mild and mellow
Would gaze about; this one was yellow.
Prompt at the stroke of nine they say
Would twinkle forth his eye of gray.

At ten, as merry as a clown,
You could behold the laughing brown.
Eleven strikes! And open flies
An eye as black as midnight skies.
And when the hour of twelve was tolled,
And Time was one more half day old,
He opened full his eye of gold.
His twelve bright eyes he flashed around
Till rainbows flecked the trees and ground!
Oh, loveliest beast in song or story,
The Wakeupworld in all his glory!

He could not sleep as others could;
But for a moment in the wood
Might stand and rest himself a mite,
Then quickly would be off in flight,
Crossing mountain, field, and lake,
Bidding the drowsy world awake.
Every hour some sleepyhead
Would hear his song and leap from bed
To open his eyes on some delight
Of lovely day or beauteous night.

What would *you* give to see alive
A Wakeupworld at half past five?
Could anything excite you more
Than seeing him at exactly four,
His eyes of white, blue, green, and red,
Leaping like carlights from his head?

[187]

Or watch each eye from hour to hour,
Beginning at exactly one,
Unfold its beauty like a flower,
Till all those eyes were on the sun?
'Twould take you half a day at least
To get the most of such a feast!
But never shall his like appear
Again, and we shall never hear
His song in lovely measures hurled
At sleepyheads throughout the world.

Excitement robbed him of his breath,
Excitement led him to his death.
Flood morning when he could have been
(Being awake) the first one in,
Excitement made him play the dunce
And open all his eyes at once!
He rushed right on through dawn and dark
Pointing late comers to the Ark.
Too great the strain was for his heart;
Slowly he sank; his great knees shook,
While those his song had helped to start
Passed on without a backward look.

The waters fell upon him there,
His twelve bright eyes shining like one;
They covered him, and none knew where
To find him when the storm was done.

The-Snake-That-Walked-Upon-His-Tail

How envied, how admired a male,
The-Snake-That-Walked-Upon-His-Tail!
The forest all emerged to stare
When he came out to take the air.
With bright eye flashing merrily,
He seemed to say, "Come, gaze on me!
Behold as near as animal's can,
A walk resembling that of man!"
And holding high his haughty head,
He would stroll on with graceful tread.
And how his tiny little ear
Would throb these compliments to hear:
"What charm he has!" "What elegance!"
"The ideal partner for a dance!"
"However do you think he learned?"
At this, although he blushed and burned
To tell them how, he never turned,
But, looking neither left nor right,
Would wander on and out of sight.

But why indeed was he so gifted?
By what strange powers was he lifted
A little nearer to the skies?
The reason's plain. Hard exercise!
Hard exercise, indeed! You shake
Your head, and think, "When did a snake,

A creature sleepy and inert,
Content to slumber in the dirt,
Or lie in caverns dank and dark,
Exhibit such a worthy spark?"

But be it found in man or horse,
(Or even snake), a driving force
The fever is we call ambition.
When it attacks, there's no condition
Of man or beast which may withstand
Ambition's hard, compelling hand.

And from his very, very birth,
No common snake was this of ours;
But he was conscious of his worth,
And well aware of all his powers.
He never cared for toads and newts,
For catching flies or digging roots;
No cavern cool could lure him in,
No muddy bank his fancy win.
Wherever man was, there was he!
Eager to watch, eager to see!
He thought it fine that Man could talk,
But finer still that Man could *walk*.
He thought, "If Man can do this, why
With proper training, so can I."

He kept his secret from his nearest
Friend, he never told his dearest,

But in a quiet glade he knew
Where none was apt to come and spy,
The more his perseverance grew,
The nearer did his dream draw nigh;
He practiced patiently and drilled,
And *wished,* and *yearned,* and *longed,* and *willed.*
From crack of dawn to darkest night,
He practiced sitting bolt upright.
At first he fell with a terrible thump,
And bruised his head and raised a bump;
But, "Walk I will!" is what he said,
And lightly rubbed his aching head.

Night after night, day after day,
He would sit up, and sway and sway,
Until one day, oh, think of it!
He stood and never swayed a bit!
He stood as rigid as a pole,
With perfect ease, perfect control!

Though Men should do most wondrous things
In years to come: on iron wings
Fly faster than the fastest bird,
Or talk or sing, and make it heard
Over mountains and over seas,
You must confess that none of these
Could for excitement quite compare
With Snake triumphant standing there
Tip-toe upon his tail! And **now**
How to begin? He wondered how!

What should he do? Leap? Jump? Or stride?
His heart was hammering inside
Its narrow cell! His throat was dry!
Ambition's fever fired his eye.
Within his grasp he had his dream.
Here was his moment, his, supreme!

Just then he chanced to glance and see
Man passing by, most leisurely;
Step after step Man took with ease,
Eclipsing houses, rocks, and trees.
And suddenly our Snake grew pale,
And whimpered forth a woeful wail;
Till Doomsday though he stood on end,
He would not walk! No need pretend!
One thing he lacked to be complete.
Nothing could walk which hadn't *feet!*

Down, down, he dropped, and sadly crept
Into a bush nearby, and wept.
The tears he shed were sad and salty;
He felt a failure, weak and faulty.
At last, too weary more to weep,
He curled him up and went to sleep.

But some sweet spirit knew his zeal,
Pitied his grief, and sped to heal.
Our Snake's ambitious lower tip
Was caught in some magician's grip,

Till where had been, so sharp and neat,
A tail, were now two tiny feet.
It may have been by wishing so
His earnestness had made them grow!
At any rate, as I repeat,
When he awoke, there were his feet!

He wept again, but now for pleasure!
His joy burst forth in lavish measure.
He popped up straighter than an arrow;
Happiness went bubbling through his marrow!

Then gingerly and cautiously,
And praying Heaven kind to be,
He put his best foot forward! Oh,
It knew exactly where to go!
Without the slightest fuss or bother
Straight behind it came the other.
And from that day until his fall,
He was a wonder to them all.

Pray notice well that last remark,
To wit: "Until his fall," for hark
How too much pride and too much glory
Bring dismal climax to our story.
Our hero, for I still opine
That such he was, though serpentine,
Waxed fat on praise and admiration,
Forgot his former lowly station,

Looked on his mate with mild disdain
As being somewhat soft of brain;
With favor viewed her not at all,
Because, poor thing, she still must *crawl*!
(Which needs no explanation here,
For we believe we've made it clear
That of these two only the Male
Contrived to walk upon his tail.)

The compliments which, left and right,
Were showered on him, spoiled him quite;
No longer friendly and benign,
He strode along with rigid spine,
Nor bent to pass the time of day
Though gently greeted on the way.
Himself he thought the world's last wonder,
All other beasts a foolish blunder,
And even Man he somewhat eyed
A bit obliquely in his pride.

One only thing, or rather two,
He loved with ardor all complete;
Yea, evermore his rapture grew
As he beheld his darling feet!
He bathed them in the coolest brooks,
Wrapped them in leaves against the heat·
He never wearied of the looks
Of those amazing little feet!
And every day, foul day or fair,
Most carefully did count his toes

To be quite certain they were there,
Two sets of five, in double rows.

Flood morning came and Mrs. Snake
Was early up and wide awake.
"Dear husband, rise," she hissed, "the Ark
We must be on and in ere dark."
But he, he only stretched and yawned,
As in his brain an idea dawned
That promised great publicity.
"Suppose, my dear, you go," said he,
"Ahead, and wait on board for me.
Your rate of travel's none too great.
You crawl along; I won't be late."

"True," said his Madam, somewhat tartly,
"I travel as the good Lord made me;
And though I may not travel smartly,
My crawling never has delayed me."
At which in somewhat of a huff,
She straightened out and rippled off.

Quite tardily our Snake arose,
Sat fondly gazing at his toes,
And thought, "The last to catch the boat
I'll be; arrive as one of note.
Perhaps its sailing I'll delay
Almost as much as one whole day;
For certainly they wouldn't dare
To sail away with me not there."

Through all the bustle and commotion
Of others hastening to the ocean,
He gayly spent his time in primping
And polishing his shiny scales,
And laughed to think of others limping
Instead of walking on their tails.

Long, long, he dillied, long, long he dallied,
And dilly-dalliers never yet
Have at the proper moment sallied
To where they were supposed to get.
At length he deemed the proper second
For his departure had appeared;
The fame of being latest beckoned;
For conquest he felt fully geared.

But even as he straightly rose,
And lightly turned upon his toes,
The quiet skies above him darkened.
A panic seized him as he harkened
To thunder rolling long and loud.
Foreboding filled his frame, and dread,
As, glancing up, he saw a cloud
About to spill its contents on his head!
He fled in fright; away he scurried;
From that disturbing spot he hurried.
Yet ever as he onward sped
That cloud still threatened overhead.

At last, at last, he nears the Ark;
'Tis just a little ways away!
Its lights are gleaming in the dark,
It rocks with laughter loud and gay.
"Oh, let me reach it," gasps our hero;
"Though fame and fortune be as zero,
Though none my praises sing aloud,
O Heaven, spare me from that cloud!"

What irony of fate is this?
What bitter fare is his to eat?
Why does our hero writhe and hiss?
Something has tangled up his feet.
A little plant, a sickly bush,
Has grappled with those lovely toes;
Though he may flounder, shove, and push,
No further on our hero goes.
The awful cloud above him tips
And pours its mighty torrents down.
One last look and the captive slips
Away within their depths to drown.
Undone by what he loved the most
He gently renders up the ghost.

Long may his mate stand at the rail,
With anxious eye explore the dark;
The-Snake-That-Walked-Upon-His-Tail
Will never walk upon the Ark.

Set in Linotype Baskerville
Format by A. W. Rushmore
Manufactured by The Haddon Craftsmen, Inc., Scranton, Pa.
Published by HARPER & BROTHERS
New York and London